Remarks On Existential Nihilism: Labelling, Narcissism and Existential Maturity.

Jack R Ernest

Copyright

Foreword

This is the fourth edition of the e-book and print edition of these notes. I have added to this edition. I have also changed some things around. I would like to make the reader aware that this book is more of social psychology or sociology than philosophy. In ways I should have called the book "Remarks on Existential Sociology" rather than that of nihilism, although the final chapter does discuss nihilism in detail.

I would also like to apologize in the third edition for singling out the female gender for criticism and to express that it was never my intention to do so. In most cases what I say can be applied to both men and women alike. In the previous edition, the chapter on love contained now regrettable remarks which have been removed in this edition. Again, I sincerely apologize for writing these things. In hindsight I was naïve.

I must also state that I repeat myself often on certain things to make it clearer for the reader to understand what I am attempting to say.

If you like this book, I would recommend you purchase the follow up to it: Remarks On Existential Sociology: The Bureaucratic Society. It can be bought on Amazon, i-tunes, google etc.

Introduction

"I know one thing and that is I know nothing." - Socrates.

We are not born narcissistic, we are not born insecure; we are taught to be narcissistic, we are taught to be insecure. This neurosis is instilled in our minds chiefly through the environment. It is the monuments of family and education that manipulate our brains when young to be insecure. As such we mature as sick beings. This narcissistic reptile becomes embedded in our conscience. Life becomes about image parameters. That we are an animal composed of trillions of atoms inhabiting a vast, yet indifferent universe is seldom realized. The narcissist only sees work and relationships. They are not aware of the universe or the mechanics of the atom. They do not see their liver or kidneys in operation, organs that are vital for existence as we know it.

My philosophy is counter intuitive. From a young age we are condemned to expose our identity to the herd through family and education. This in turn creates anxiety which is neutralized through conforming. But as I allude to in these notes, in conforming or at least in yearning to conform, we are attacked with anxiety again. One of the ways to overcome this angst is to defy what the economic system demands. So, one limits their exposure to the greater world in order to become more secure in their being. The problem is (and this is most certainly the case for the narcissistic individual) one is conditioned to expose their identity to the tribe. Thus, such an individual instinctively permutes that they need to know people in order to be happy. If they should fall out with a friend, they simply remark that they will find a new friend. If they fall out with a co-worker, they simply remark that they will get a new job. Thus, the individual is perpetually of the belief that they need to know people in order to be happy and as such are blind to the fact that it is the very people that know them, that make them insecure. In my opinion the current economic environment that is adopted by mankind, makes one insecure and to be truly liberated one must be anonymous.

The goal of these notes is to make people existentially mature because such maturity is in my opinion a more concrete method to live. Those who are mature appreciate the world. They are not corrupted by the narcissistic template that drowns them in self-obsession. The mature of this world recognise the enormous chance that they are alive. They see how lucky they are to be a member of a species that exerts such dominance over the world as we know it. They see past the economic system that makes people anxious and thus live more fulfilling lives.

The primary influences on my philosophy are Erving Goffman, RD Laing, Irvin Yalom and Rollo May. I am also extremely influenced by social psychology, sociology, the Stoics and Buddhism.

"You can hold yourself back from the sufferings of the world, that is something you are free to do and it accords with your nature, but perhaps this very holding back is the one suffering you could avoid." – Franz Kafka.

Chapter One

Language

"The limits of my language mean the limits of my world." - Ludwig Wittgenstein.

We are human because we can articulate and not the other way around.

Man is an animal with the advantage of language. Language is to the conscience what light is to the eye. Language is the light of civilization.

Language and labelling are strongly associated with each other. That we can use language means we can label in a rather unusual method. The animal that lacks language is not afforded this luxury. From the labelling then stems the Labelling Anxiety and from that comes the Capitalistic Insecurity. But the focal point of these things is language.

Without language we would only be able to label in the same method as the animal without language can.

It is because one is devoured with language when young, that they can be inveigled by language when older. Henceforth this is why good speaking is adored by the majority and a requirement when selling a product be it a technology or oneself.

We expect to be enthralled by conversation with co-workers. We expect to be wooed by the politician who speaks well. We expect to be satisfied by the sales representative who wishes us to buy a product.

It is just ample use of psychology to influence a mind whose apex is language. Language is thus the addiction of the masses. It is how the majority gets its high. Language is the currency of human existence.

Language conditions us to talk on cue and not to think. People spend far too much time talking and getting narcotized on the language of others that they refuse to think lucidly about what they say or what they do. It becomes an addiction and thus one can see why socialization is a huge faculty of what we call life. We are damned to speak, but how many people can enjoy their own silence?

How a person speaks is the greatest indicator of their personality because they rely on instinct to answer.

One does not do something unless there is gain from it. One does not exercise unless you gain physically or perhaps mentally. This is why language is glorified throughout human civilization. It makes the listener and the talker feel good about themselves. Life is both solidified and made chaotic through language.

It becomes like a film or book in that it serves as an organ to entertain an individual. But for what it affords us in one department it takes in another. One cannot conceive rationally when one is unconsciously instructed to respond in nanoseconds to a question.

"One does not inhabit a country; one inhabits a language. That is our country, our fatherland - and no other." - Emil Cioran.

The people live on instinct and not reason and this instinct is unconscious conformity. What is a man without friendship and freedom they ask? What is a man without language I ask? Man is cursed to talk. We live in a world wherein we must converse. We must argue. Existence knows of no other way to live.

Men are prepared to expend their existence in following, at the expense of leading themselves. They converse with others and stalk their own shadows.

So, the very qualities that are demanded of us by our peers (good interpersonal skills) are actually the very skills that incarcerate us to the will of others.

Through concise articulation one becomes a pervert of conformity. Through being preoccupied with others and their language we sell ourselves and rarely question what we do. We then wake up on a rainy Monday morning in the twilight of our lives and wonder did we make the correct choices in life and by then it is too late to recover what we so delicately let go.

A by-product of socialization is the infatuation with marriage. Good communication skills are in part one of the drivers of conformity.

Language generates all these concepts that we endeavour to follow unconsciously. We overcomplicate life with language. Life is simple really: We exist, and we are a slave to our addictions. If you could rewind the dominos of all genius and tyranny, the first domino is boredom and the second is language.

We can seek meaning only because we speak. Take away language and we would be like all other animals hopelessly lost in a struggle to maintain survival. What has happened though is because we can speak, we have formulated the economic system as a means to negotiate existence. But this economic system in turn blinds us to the realities of existence that using language births. Life to this sick narcissist becomes about love and work when the nihilistic truth is there is no motivation to live. But one can still be grateful despite the despair.

Not god and not because we are human, but because we can speak is the reason we perceive the world as we do.

"Man acts as though he were the shaper and master of language, while in fact language remains the master of man." – Martin Heidegger.

The obvious question to ask yourself is: Does god exist independent of man? But a more stimulating question to ask is: Does god exist independent of language? The atheists remark that if there was no universe and hence no man, there would be no such thing as god. True, no doubt, but a more damning indictment of religion is if you deprived mankind of the ability to speak, there too would be no such thing as god. God like true love is something we have concocted not because we are intelligent but because we can speak. God is language.

We are intelligent because we can speak and not the other way around.

Addiction

"Every form of addiction is bad, no matter whether the narcotic be alcohol, morphine or idealism." – Carl Jung.

We are all addicts, but addictions that aid an economy are considered both necessary and normal.

Conversation is an addiction. A good conversation makes us feel good just as alcohol or sex does.

We are slaves to gratification. We are dopamine addicts. One other thing we are addicted to is the addiction to being labelled correctly. When we are labelled positively by society, we feel content. Thus, people are seduced by labels; by the chance to accrue an appropriate label.

We use gratification to defuse the demons of the absurd. But we become too addicted to being gratified. What Buddhism or Stoicism tutors one to do is to become one with the universe. Make being alive your gratification.

Maybe if we were not so addicted to other people (being approved by them) we could actually feel a semblance of happiness. If we were not so addicted to being labelled correctly by them, we would have more freedom.

Conformity is the addiction of the moralistic. They are addicted to being labelled positively. They then use conversation, food, sex, sports teams, films, books, etc. as a means to be gratified.

It is when we are most alive that we are most addicted. The life of the early adult is one of inebriation. They are addicted to sex, image, money, love, conversation etc. It is only when they grow old, do they find peace.

The one thing we are also addicted to but never realize is positive affirmation from our peers. When we are endorsed by an individual or by a group, we feel good. Thus, this is the reason why a woman tries to look attractive; she gains endorsement. This is also the reason why men try to be successful; he gains commendation. It also explains why so many marry or form relationships because the symbol of their relationship or marriage induces validation from their peers. This is a commoditized relationship. So, when you rewind back the dominos even further you will realize that the true instigator of relationships/marriage is fear. We are afraid of what people will think of us and therefore try to earn their ratification. We are afraid to be seen alone or to be perceived as a failure.

Now the thing to remember about all those addictions, is that they are operated with respect to another person or persons. By this I mean a vital part of the addiction is a dependence on another individual or individuals to approbate you. For example, you need to speak to another person, you tidy up your appearance to impress another person, you make love to another person and you try to earn the approval of another person or persons. So basically, the average individual is so reliant on another person or persons to be happy and this is why there are so many unhappy people alive in this universe, because when they are not psychologically approved by these people they are dependent on, they become unhappy. The goal of Existential Nihilistic Therapy or at least one of them is to endeavour to make the individual cut ties with another person or persons for their self-esteem. In other words, to not worry about what others think of them because life in reality is too great to possess such worries.

We are all impulsive addicts. But the addiction to image or to appeasing the herd is ascertained by the herd to be satisfactory.

People will look at the Tibetan monks with scorn. "They deprive themselves of gratification. Isn't that what life is about." But these monks have life figured out. They are not addicted to gratification but rather they are addicted to their own existence, their own place in this universe. I observe society and all I see are desperate addicts. Men and women are addicted to sex, to image, to appeasing the herd, to avoiding boredom, to conversation, to drugs, to fighting, to religions, to sports teams and more. They use all these things to fuel their addictive happiness. They are hooked on these qualities to make life worthwhile, to banish the reptilian absurdness to the abyss. It seems that to be alive in this universe is no match for the capitalistic nature of society. Consequently, they pour all their money and waste all their time in being emotionally gratified. Thus, to be free in this world is to be free of addiction. In other words, make being alive your sole gratification.

Why doesn't psychiatry recognise the brainwashing of society? They do not because this is how society is channelled into providing for an economy. Love and work said Sigmund Freud. It should be love yourself in this universe and work in a job that makes you happy, not one that makes you money.

It is not enough as an intelligent species to simply persevere in this universe. In order to be happy, we must live this dream life we are supposed to live. We must have the partner, the family, the house, the stellar job and more. Why do we think like this? We do so because we have through childhood and other factors been programmed to think like this. This is narcissism polluting our conscience. Furthermore, we want to be labelled correctly and through conforming we acquire this positive label. Being labelled positively has a huge influence on why we conform.

For example, no one ever questions why they drive on the correct side of the road or stop at the red lights. They do these things unconsciously because they have been taught by society to behave this way. These rules then become unconsciously impregnated into the mind of the individual and one performs them on instinct. They become familiar to us, as the Mere Exposure Theory says. Then if they disavow these rules they become negatively labelled. They are controlled by both the fact that they are brainwashed to behave a precise way and also through the threat of being labelled.

To be free of addiction is to be free.

Americans have a drug problem; they are addicted to the American Dream.

Whenever we feel bored, we instinctively seek out conversation or food or sex etc. This is why we never achieve much. Our addictions are universal.

Life is the most important drug you need to be addicted to.

Addiction is the mainstay of the human condition. The common man is addicted to being common. He is addicted to being labelled appropriately.

Capitalism wants addicts. It wants society to be addicted to conversation, to sex, to image, to appeasing the herd because when you add up all these addictions you get a functioning economy.

Boredom must be thought of as a form of pain that we are devoted to avoiding.

The films of Michelangelo Antonioni truly capture the alienation of life. Life is boring and that is why we use cinema, sports, relationships, work etc. as a means to be gratified.

We can't understand the religious fanatics, yet we have no issue falling in love or supporting the sports team. All three are just examples of the power of manipulation.

Everything is an elopement from the death anxiety and boredom. Friendships, sports, sex, conversation, image etc. are your capitalistic morphine.

Labelling

"When you label me, you negate me." - Soren Kierkegaard.

Man is damned to be labelled. Traditional sociologists only apply labelling theory to the criminals. The reality is that it should be applied to everyone.

The price one must pay for living (choosing) is that we become labelled.

How you are labelled is a component of your psyche.

The Labelling Phenomenon: We are always analysing our environment. We are at all times labelling what we see. We are labelling people; they in turn are labelling us. We are dividing things into positive or negative; acceptable or unacceptable; appropriate or inappropriate. This is done with people but also with other things such as cars driving on the road. You have Conscious Labelling and Unconscious Labelling. Conscious Labelling is labelling someone a friend or a deviant. Unconscious Labelling is when you are labelling those you do not know but interact with, such as walking up a street in a city. Despite the fact you do not know these people, you are labelling their behaviour. But it is unconscious, so you do not realize you are labelling them.

The Labelling Anxiety: We fear being negatively labelled. It could be people we know or people we don't know. This fear of being negatively labelled controls our behaviour. We strive to retrieve or maintain a positive label. We strive to avoid a negative label.

The Labelling Bind: Because of the Labelling Anxiety we get coerced, influenced or manipulated into doing certain things. We may not want to do something, but the threat of a negative label makes us do that certain something. For example, a friend invites you out. But you do not wish to go. However, because you realize that if you do not go, your friend will think you are rude and hence will negatively label you, you are compelled to go, to avoid this negative label.

The Labelling Chain Reaction. Being known (labelled by one person) can make us be labelled by more people. Being known by people, leads to being known by more people, which in turn leads to fearing being negatively labelled by these new people. For example, we fear a negative label from a friend who invites us out (Labelling Anxiety). This motivates us to meet up with this friend, even though we do not want to (Labelling Bind). Then when we meet up with this friend, we may get introduced to even more people and so begins a cycle or pattern, whereby we repeat the Labelling Anxiety and Labelling Bind with these new people.

The Labelling Conflict: Often there is a clash between desire (and other things) and being labelled. One wants sex but can be negatively labelled because of it. The woman who is promiscuous gets negatively labelled. The same applies to the hunt for money, in that it can lead to a bad reputation. The man who sells drugs to earn a living, gets labelled a criminal. Or maybe someone has unique views, which when expressed, lead to a negative label by society. Or maybe a latent homosexual is afraid to disclose his sexuality because he fears a negative label from family and friends.

When you become known, you become labelled and thus try to be emotionally vindicated by the person who knows you. You become caged by their opinion of you. You lose your freedom and commit existential suicide.

When you know someone (perhaps a co-worker) and they know you, you are put under pressure by them. Now apply this logic to family and friends. They put us under duress to behave a certain way.

The female in order to receive positive verification from the male must be attractive. The male in order to receive positive verification from the female must be attractive. What they don't realize is that their behaviour is unconsciously influenced by the herd. They live to placate the herd; to be positively labelled by the herd because they feel good when they are. Thus, to be known is to be condemned. Thus, there is no such thing as a positive label. Thus, people are not free.

Our unconscious mind is working round the clock. All behaviour is being divided into positive/acceptable/appropriate or negative/unacceptable/inappropriate. We do this even with people we do not know.

Men and women both command each other. Men in order to receive positive affirmation from a girlfriend or wife must concede. They must repress their instinctive drive. Women too must adapt to propitiate the boyfriend or husband. Through labelling, society regulates the individual and the individual regulates society.

A lot of our happiness and despair is linked to labelling. A man may want the woman of his dreams to like him, which is another way of saying he wants her to positively endorse him. Imagine for instance then that this said man rapes the woman. Now she negatively labels him. Our lives are lost in a battle of labels and it is a battle we cannot win.

I don't think we realize that everyone we meet is another individual who sociologically incarcerates us.

The Labelling Phenomenon is like space time. Gravity according to Einstein is not a force but is simply matter warping the fabric of spacetime. Likewise, society controls society through labelling. When you are walking up a busy street, you are controlling the behaviour of the people you see through labelling; they in turn are controlling you through labelling also. The very fact that you see them and they you, controls both you and them. But you cannot see this mechanism, only its response.

We understand physical violence. But what of psychological violence? What if knowing people was violence upon your conscience? We conform because of psychological violence in the form of being labelled.

Being known is in fact violence upon our conscience, much like if we came face to face with a lion that has not eaten in a week. We are continuously being bombarded with one's interpretation of us.

In much the same vein that traffic accidents are caused by the close proximity of cars to each other, psychological violence is caused by people knowing each other. Every person that knows you, interprets you and this interpretation is a form of malice upon your conscience.

As long as you affiliate yourself with the herd you deprive yourself of your freedom. We are all gods and devils. It's just a matter of interpretation.

We tie our self-esteem to being endorsed by the herd be it our friends, family or facebook.

How much do men and women spend on trying to make themselves look desirable? The reason why 99.9% of men and women will die and be forgotten is that they measure success in being desired.

We instinctively label the hermetic individual who keeps to himself as odd. We instinctively label the person in love as normal. This has a powerful ramification on society. They wish to be labelled positively by the herd and how do they achieve this feat? Through being in a relationship. It is not burned into your DNA that you need to get married. This is something we have concocted because we can speak and so many honestly believe that the substance for life is to fall in love. They unconsciously attest that they must be in a relationship to be valued or to be of worth.

We deliberately label the dysfunctional as outcasts. This in turn promotes conformism. People are too afraid to go alone. Schizoid PD for example isn't really a personality disorder but can be thought of as a different mentality.

How many of society tie their happiness to image. When they look good, they in turn feel good. So, a man who earns a hundred grand a year, immediately feels content about such a proposition. And the woman who deems herself sexy, immediately feels good because she is attractive. Their happiness is contingent on depicting a positive image to the herd.

Theory of interpretation: The world will never be perfect as long as we interpret it. It is our interpretations that make the world positive or negative and not the world itself.

Interpretation: Punch someone on the street and you get sent to jail. Violently beat the opposing individual in a boxing match and you get a gold-plated belt. The same event is being interpreted differently because the conditions have changed slightly. This is the Interpretation Contradiction. Another example is how we can murder another person in the name of war, yet we cannot murder someone when not engaged in war.

Out of our recklessness to control society we have given birth to criminality. Given man's inhumanity, the only means of eradicating crime is if you abolish the law.

"The looking glass self," was the term coined by sociologist Charles Horton Cooley. It expresses the tendency for one to understand oneself through their own understanding of the perception which others may hold of them.

There are three main components that comprise the looking-glass self:

We imagine how we must appear to others.

We imagine and react to what we feel their judgment of that appearance must be.

We develop our self through the judgments of others.

The judiciary is a game of interpretation. It is one's interpretation versus another.

Everything is interpretation.

There are no laws; everything is permitted. But society has adopted a system of economic stability in favour of anarchy.

You are as much a potential perpetrator as you are a potential victim. It depends on how you are labelled.

The criminal is labelled. He is afraid to be recognised because of this label. But the law-abiding citizen is afraid also. He or she is afraid of being potentially labelled.

The sociological fallout or by product of interaction is crime. When we interact with someone, that interaction is interpreted by the receiver. They either declare it to be positive or negative and if it is negative, we call that interaction a crime. Thus, it stands to reason that if you wish to limit crime, limit interaction. Yet the authorities would never dream of such an Orwellian world because we need people to interact so that the economic system can prevail.

Imagine the phenomenon when you walk down a street and recognise someone you know. If you analyse this interaction, you can learn so much. The second you recognise that person, your mind thinks to acknowledge them. So, you say "hello," and perhaps stop to chat to them. Why don't you just walk by them without acknowledging them? Why don't you do this with people you do not know? We want to be labelled positively; we strive often unconsciously to avoid a negative label. It is this recognition phenomenon (this labelling mechanism) that is defective in schizophrenia.

It gets interesting when you analyse Unconscious Labelling. Unconscious Labelling is where you are labelling those you do not even know. Such as people in a crowd at a rock concert. Now imagine that this labelling process is defective. It is malfunctioning. This is a part of schizophrenia I theorize. The way they label other people, whether they know them or not, is defective.

We are hypnotised by labels. Food, clothes and technology are the obvious ones. We need to buy specific brands to feel gratified. The less obvious ones are relationships and careers. This is the commoditization of our lives that consumes us. We need to be seen in a relationship and working a certain job just so we can be covertly approved by people we do not care about.

The Labelling Anxiety is like space-time applied to society. It always manipulates the individual . "If I do this, how will I be labelled?" It is a phenomenon in both the individual and society. Being known warps the behaviour of the individual at all times. The individual responds to society. They respond to the potential threat of being negatively labelled. They walk up a street and do not run up one because of labelling, because of being known. When we interact with society, we either positively label that interaction or negatively label it. Positive labelling is often unconscious, in that we do not realize we have positively labelled someone. Again, you walk up a street and do not run because you wish to be positively labelled by people you do not even know.

Labelling Anxiety: Imagine you are walking up a street with people walking in the opposite direction to you, as in they are walking against you. Now you do not know any of these people. Imagine now for instance three people who are walking against you stop, turn around and start running in the opposite direction they were originally walking. This is immediately labelled adversely by you. You then look behind you and see that a man is carrying a gun. But it is the fact that these people initially behaved in a way that you negatively labelled that caught your attention and these are people you do not know. The point I am trying to make is that even as you walk by people you do not know, you are all the time dividing their behaviour into Acceptable or Positive and Unacceptable or Negative. Again, a lot of this positive behaviour is only registered unconsciously. It is only when someone acts odd (negatively) that you register it consciously.

When you stand around waiting for a bus with other strangers, you may not know them, but you are labelling them. Their behaviour is always divided into Acceptable/Unacceptable. As I assert, Acceptable behaviour is only registered by the unconscious. But should one member of that group behave erratically, he or she will become negatively labelled. For example, if one person took off all his or her clothes, he or she will be negatively labelled. But the important thing to remember is that they were positively labelled by everyone despite not being aware that they were labelled.

Being known is psychological assault on our mind. We do not perceive the assault, but we respond to it. So, when you are walking down the street and see someone you know, you instinctively think to say hello to them. Saying "hello" to them is the response to the assault. Likewise, when you walk down a busy city street and pass by people you do not know, you again respond to this assault by these people you do not know. So, you walk at a certain pace and avoid banging into these people. That is again how you respond to the assault you do not actually perceive. Now imagine this assault from being known is malfunctioning. How would it manifest itself? I theorize it would manifest itself by what we call schizophrenia. Schizophrenia in my opinion is just an adverse response to this psychological assault.

We fear a bear we meet in the woods. Likewise, we fear society, through them knowing us. Their interpretation of us is violence upon our conscience.

This assault, which is interpretation, which in actuality is how we are labelled, shapes or moulds society as much as desire or money or religion.

I wonder if alien life from another star system or even galaxy would be able to distinguish between us. Would we all look the same and behave the same to them or would they like us humans do distinguish between different types of people.

When people acknowledge us positively, we feel good. Thus, we tie our self-happiness to how we are labelled by those who perceive us.

Being known is both at once the venom and the mania of existence. When the people who know us approve of us, they make us feel worthy; but those who demean us, they make life unbearable.

The modern-day man and woman are under severe burden to be the modern-day man and woman. They are addicted to being labelled fittingly. This is why in part we chase relationships and professional careers. We want to be labelled positively by the herd, ergo our peers. This is most certainly the case with insecure people who are narcissistic.

You date not just because you just enjoy it but because you also gain pleasure from pacifying the herd. That you can convey to your peers that you are in a relationship makes you feel good.

We do so much in life just to be approved.

Existence is a crime; opinion is the punishment. We fear one's interpretation of us more than their fists.

Fame and criminality are the two extremes of being known.

We fear opinions more than guns. The criminal must fear bullets; the law-abiding individual must fear interpretation. Being known influences your behaviour. We are afraid of being known and we don't realize it, but we unconsciously respond to it.

Your life is what you interpret it to be.

Fame debases like no other. We are blind in the dark; but equally so we are blind when we stare at the sun.

Fame is as much a venom as it is an aphrodisiac. Success is often the failure.

Banking on fame making you happy is like jumping off a bridge and expecting to fly. Fame is a fickle friend.

A lot of anxiety stems from our peers, ergo those who know us. Now imagine you were famous, and your peers are the whole world. It explains why so many famous people commit suicide. They just can't handle being known by everyone.

To be known by friends and family means we must acknowledge them or validate them. To be known by the whole world means we must authenticate the whole world.

An individual is either loved, despised or worst ignored.

I once heard a journalist say: "Real men don't visit prostitutes." In other words, they get married to achieve sexual fulfilment. But this is wrong. This version of men is from the perspective of the female majority and what they want the ideal man to do. It's like saying real women aren't overweight. This ideal woman that society idolizes is in turn the viewpoint of the male. We use the married man and woman as the template for society.

Man is the only animal that can be shamed.

Life is often a case of one's interpretation versus another's.

If you think of how fame corrupts and then apply that principle to the individual who is ordinary but has friends, co-workers, parents and a partner, you begin to understand the anxiety that torments man.

There is no such thing as a positive label because the very act of being labelled means that we become both controlled and condemned. Take a husband and wife for instance. The husband is labelled by the wife and must continue to fulfil obligations to remain a husband, as must the wife. They both must adjust their behaviour to accommodate the interpretation of the other.

There is a conflict between being known and desire. There also exists a conflict between being known and earning money. What I am trying to convey is that if you take sexual desire, a man for instance visits escorts to fulfil himself, but this desire exposes him to negative labelling. Likewise, with money, we need to work to earn a living, yet this working exposes us again to potential labelling from co-workers and bosses. Being known is existential suicide because we become afraid of the interpretation of those who know us.

Labelling is a unique element of being human. We do not label an animal a murderer or a genius. The animal is simply an animal responding to stimulus. With humans, we do label. In fact, every human we interact with is labelled. This labelling is the source of so much anxiety and woe. Very often the individual with low self-esteem yearns to be labelled more positively in life.

Society does not realize that the more they associate themselves within society the more damned they become.

A neurotic person fears being negatively labelled. What we define a healthy individual is one that is seduced by the chance of accruing a positive label. For example, the neurotic fears the next day at work because he or she fears doing something wrong and hence becomes negatively labelled. The healthy individual in contrast looks forward to getting a new job because he or she sees it as something they can build their life on. They are seduced by the reward of a positive label.

The healthy individual is so conditioned to man that they do not see him as a menace.

If we all wore masks, life would be much simpler. Suicide is being known.

Anonymity is freedom.

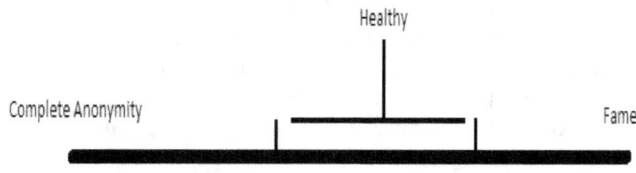

Fig 1: *Too much fame and too much anonymity can be detrimental to one's mental health.*

"I knew a man who was blind. When he was nearly 40 years old he had an operation and regained his sight…. At first he was elated, really high—faces, colours, landscapes. But then everything began to change. The world was much poorer than he had imagined. No one had ever told him how much dirt there was, how much ugliness. He noticed ugliness everywhere. When he was blind, he used to cross the street alone with a stick. After he regained his sight, he became afraid, he began to live in darkness, he never left his room. After three years he killed himself." - The Passenger (A film by Michelangelo Antonioni).

We are dictating each other's behaviour and we do not realize it. We do not want to be negatively labelled and thus try to appease the other individual(s). This applies to a relationship or society overall.

Once man exposes himself to the world, he becomes known and in becoming known he is damned.

The only way one can be totally free is to not be known because when they are not known they are not labelled. Alas the economic system kills this. Within the current economic system, we are compelled to socialize.

If you analyse suicide amongst people, I will wager that being negatively labelled had a huge bearing in the suicide. Perhaps the individual fell out with friends or a lover; perhaps the individual kept viewing his or herself as a failure. Those are simply different ways of saying they are negatively labelled and wish to be positively labelled.

We live in a labelling culture.

The Labelling Phenomenon is one of the reasons we are distracted from the universe. When you interact with people, regardless of whether you know them or not, you are so preoccupied with labelling that you do not have time to think otherwise. Apply this to friendship, to work, to walking up a busy city street by yourself. In all three of those things, you seldom think about the nature of the universe or the complexity of the atom. All three things have distracted you, through (in part) the Labelling Anxiety. You are so preoccupied with managing your interaction with these people, that the true nature of the world is a distant thought.

Your enthusiasm to be labelled positively is just another way of saying you fear being labelled negatively.

Your freedom involves many things. One of the essential needs is that you outgrow this Labelling Anxiety. Unfortunately, most people do not mature out of the phase until they grow old. The trick is to be mature as an adult when you are young.

You may conclude that when you walk up a busy city street or sit in a lecture theatre in college, that you are just ignoring all the people around you, whether you know them or not. The reality is that you do acknowledge them. You are always labelling their behaviour, as they are you. Basically, you are afraid of them, you are afraid of being negatively labelled by them, you are afraid of being laughed by them, but it is often unconscious. This is why in part you conform, because it is a means to neutralize the threat of being adversely labelled. That is the Labelling Anxiety. This is why you behave a precise way because you know this is how society will positively label you. Now two things to ponder: A) You are not afraid of what animals think of you, only humans. You may fear a bear in that it may attack you, but you are not afraid of being laughed at by that said bear. This is a trait that exists solely in humans because we can use language to label in another way. B) What if this whole process by which you label is malfunctioning? What if it was defective? This is why I theorize that labelling is a part of schizophrenia.

You are interacting with everyone, even those you do not know, through labelling them. You are always splitting events into appropriate/inappropriate. Imagine sitting in a coffee shop minding your own business and there are other people doing the same, people you do not know. You are interacting with them because you are labelling how they behave, often unconsciously. So long as they all keep to themselves, you pay no attention to them, as in you unconsciously label their behaviour as appropriate. But if one person started shouting in a negative manner, you would then consciously label that behaviour and hence person as inappropriate.

Exposure to the herd is a psychological assault upon your identity. This is part of how you are manipulated into instinctively thinking about being in a relationship. Now you do not perceive the assault and nor do you often perceive the response. You just instinctively react to this assault by thinking of behaving a certain way.

The more we expose ourselves to the herd, the more we are compelled to adopt the herds ideology. Exposure manipulates your decision process. Why does everyone think of being in a relationship? They do in part because of this exposure to the herd. Be it education or work, when we embroil ourselves with other people, we seek to be labelled positively by them and to do this we need to be in a relationship. Thus, to mature one must overcome this persuasion.

There is a link between being sociable and wanting to be in a relationship. Socialization enforces a relationship upon you.

When using an anonymous alias on an internet forum we fear our real identity being discovered. Now one must apply that fear to the real world of interaction. When we interact with people, we always fear their interpretation of us. We thus try to be endorsed by them and they by us. They control our behaviour and we in turn control theirs. When they approve of us, we feel good, but when they dismiss us, we feel bad. It stands to reason that if one truly wishes to be free, they would be advised to live alone and avoid everyone. In living in seclusion, they cannot be interpreted and hence controlled. Furthermore, they do not rely on another's approval to be of esteem.

To rid the world of evil, rid the world of man, because without man and man's interpretation there is no geniuses or monsters, no good or bad. The animal cannot interpret and that is why there is no evil in the animal kingdom.

Is the world imperfect because people do evil things or is it because we can interpret those evil doings as evil? There are no criminals in the animal kingdom. The foundations of good and bad are at the behest of man's interpretation.

If you are different you will be labelled.

We are obsessed with being labelled appropriately through obtaining the correct labels or a precise image. A man needs the correct watch, the correct clothes, the correct hairstyle, the correct car and not surprisingly the correct woman. He treats his partner as a mechanism of which to gain a distinguished label. This is not love; this is a commoditized relationship. Now the female of society does the same thing. Why do some females crave the man in high demand? They do so because when they are seen attached to one, they get labelled positively by their peers. Labelling (the reward of a positive label) has such a huge psychological influence on our decision making. If the individual improves our image (how we are labelled by the herd) we have a good chance of choosing the individual to be our partner.

You understand the power of labelling when someone commits a crime. What you do not see is the power of labelling done by friends, family and co-workers.

Marrying someone for a good label is nothing more than a marriage of convenience.

Conventional sociology says that unless you commit a crime, you are not labelled at all by the herd (society). This is not true. Even those who have not committed crime, still get labelled negatively by society. Take the plight of famous people and apply it to the non-famous individual. Then you must also factor in that a positive label is actually a negative label in that we become controlled by the person who positively labels us.

A nuclear holocaust or a chemical warfare isn't our biggest fear. Our biggest fear is that people will not like us. Thus, our daily existence is plagued with this fear and hence we do so much to try and get people to approve of us.

We are always unconsciously saying to ourselves: If I am seen with this (be it a person or a house or a piece of clothing), how will the herd interpret me? Your mind is frequently asking this question. What it conveys is that ultimately you are afraid of what people think of you and as such try to engineer your projection in such a way that you are validated.

It is a very fragile world we inhabit because we are constantly being bombarded by one's interpretation of us. We are always trying to maintain a positive label.

Laughter is often the sculptor of society.

Once known you are labelled and cruelly damned. Sartre said man is condemned to choose. The by-product of choice is being labelled. Man, thus is condemned to be labelled.

Ross Lockridge Jr who wrote a best seller in Raintree County (and became famous) committed suicide due to the pressures of fame. He committed suicide due to the pressure of being known. "I walk past people," he confided to his wife, "and I wonder what they think." Being labelled is the sum of all our fears. But we are in a bind in that we are forced to advertise our identity to the herd. So, what we instinctively do to neutralize this angst is conform.

It is well known that Truman Capote's greatest achievement and greatest failure was his book In Cold Blood. The success of that book ultimately killed him.

I remember reading an article about a man who won the lotto and he said it destroyed him and that he wished he had never won it. He said that because of his fame after winning it, people started looking for money and suing him. Again, this provides more fuel to my theory that being known is not a luxury, but a hindrance.

Why doesn't the female of society cut her hair short? What is motivating the hordes of women to conform to have long hair? Well look at it like this: What happens if a woman decides to have short hair? She gets labelled negatively by her peers. Her parents, her friends and her co-workers will speak negatively about her. She will no longer be deemed attractive to the male of society. This negative labelling is just another way of saying she is afraid of what people think of her. Thus, to be free in an existential method is to dissolve this fear. It is to approach life in a released method. Aim to be an existential criminal but within the law.

"Do not live to satisfy the expectations of others" - Ichiro Kishimi

No reputation is better than a bad reputation. To be unknown is better than to be convicted.

Get rid of the labels because when you do that you get rid of the segregation. No whites or blacks; no men or women; no heterosexual or homosexual. Just intelligent individuals lighting bright fires in this dark landscape.

Through labelling society regulates the individual which in turn regulates society itself.

Being known is assault on our conscience. Just as if someone hit you with their fist, that is physical assault, when someone sees you, they attack you with their interpretation of you. How your mind reacts to that assault determines your psychology.

Interaction is the silent invisible moulder of society. Labelling shapes our behaviour. We behave in such a way as to be labelled positively. Essentially, we fear being known.

Conformity, narcissism and schizophrenia are in ways, three different responses to being known, to being labelled.

Forgiveness, don't make me laugh, once known, you can never be forgiven.

The battlefield is the streets of the secure western society; the battleground is the hearts of the moralistic.

Now I see no resolution to this dilemma or insecurity. Such is the economic system that we are born to parents, then educated and then must work and these three things control our behaviour and hence make us conform because they make us insecure. But do not doubt me when I say, that if you can distance yourself from these three things, you can become much more secure and hence happy in your existence. But given the current economic system, being emotionally secure and being financially secure are often mutually exclusive.

Man can be everything except nothing.

Schizoid and Avoidant are both influenced by the threat of being labelled. The avoidant fears being negatively labelled. For example, they fear being called ugly or short or fat or unintelligent and so on. The schizoid on the other hand is not afraid of being slandered so to speak. The schizoid fears exposure of his identity to the other. It is more of an existential threat.

Given the current economic system, interaction is a necessity, but this interaction is a source of angst for the individual. So how do we negotiate this anxiety? We use the myth of true love to neutralize the anxiety in being in a relationship with someone. That we can love and be loved overwhelms the anxiety of being known. With work we use the reward of money to counter the threat of being known. Earning money pulverises this existential threat. Both love and money are a means to seduce the individual so that they will adopt the system.

A large part of the reason why we have so many conformists and so few rebels is that people are rattled. They are afraid to go alone through this world. They are afraid of what their parents, friends and co-workers will say about them.

We are condemned to choose and henceforth condemned to be labelled. The only way you cannot be labelled is if you cannot choose and the only way you can't choose is if you are not alive.

You must remember that in today's world even the person you love has the potential to be a journalist.

Collective interpretation is what controls society.

The battle of minorities is a battle of labelling. They fight to be positively labelled. The crisis of failure is often a crisis of labelling.

My advice is do the opposite to what the system has taught you. From a young age you are taught to interact and to expose your identity to people. My philosophy is limit this exposure. Limit how many people know you and become happy in the silence.

We are in an all-out war of interpretation. We are constantly being bombarded with threats of labelling.

Through labelling and the threat of a potential negative label, society reaches a sort of equilibrium. You can see the equilibrium when walking in a busy city street. Everyone makes adjustments to not bump into each other. Everyone walks up the street and does not run. They cross the road when it is clear to do so. Labelling is shaping how they behave. Of course, when something negative happens, it disrupts this equilibrium. If for example a car crashes into a pedestrian, we negatively label that event. Or if someone took off all their clothes or attacked someone, again the equilibrium is disrupted

When the equilibrium is disturbed, we send the guilty party off to prisons, psychiatric hospitals, we write about them in the papers, we laugh at them and we stigmatize them.

The man is addicted to sex; the woman, to being labelled in love.

The existential paradox is this: It is the people you love who you fear.

Labelling is how you discipline society.

Men and women both make each other hate each other. They both make each other insecure. I see this repeatedly in relationships. A woman for example, does not just pick the person she likes. She calibrates whether her friends and family will like him also. She is influenced by the judgement of her peerage. She instinctively says: "If I bring this guy home to mammy and daddy, will they be impressed? Or if I bring him out to meet my friends, will they be intrigued?" She is warped by the herd. The herd is dictating her behaviour, her decision process. This is the cusp of the Labelling Anxiety. We wish to be labelled positively because when we are, we feel good. We are just so afraid of the tribe. Men do the same.

A relationship by default gives birth to the Labelling Anxiety and hence the Labelling Bind. Both the male and female (or perhaps two males/females) become anxious at the thought of losing the relationship. This is the Labelling Anxiety. To neutralize this anxiety, they conform to their partners wishes. This is the Labelling Bind. An obvious example is the female fears her husband not finding her attractive anymore (Labelling Anxiety) and so must continue to try to remain as attractive as possible (Labelling Bind). Likewise, the husband must continue to work to earn money so his wife will stay with him. The same mechanism can be applied to friendship or work relations. We all the time must behave a certain way to maintain a positive label.

To truly love you must violate the tribe.

The insecure are so addicted to being labelled appropriately that it confines them to immaturity. Their whole journey of existence becomes one of labelling gratification and not one of sincere enjoyment. They marry, they work, they conduct themselves all so they can be positively labelled by their peerage. To escape this wrath of labelling is to mature.

Imagine how uncomfortable it would be if everyone knew each other. Imagine for instance walking down a street and you recognise everyone, and they recognise you; you would almost feel like a criminal in such a situation. This is the threat of being known. Thus, there are two states: One in which we are known and one in which we are anonymous, and you need a bit of both to be secure. But too much of any one state can be detrimental.

To be existentially mature you must rid yourself of this Labelling Anxiety.

To be known is to be condemned and to be condemned is to be known. You can only label someone if you know them. The more known you are, the more you risk being labelled.

Why on the internet do escorts hide their faces and married women do not? When you understand that proposition you can understand labels.

Recognition is an event horizon that cannot be reversed. Once known, you are condemned.

The naïve view is to understand that we are under pressure from the opposite sex. So men behave as men to impress women and vice versa. That is true but it is only part of it. We are also persuaded by parents, by friends and by co-workers. They do have a say in how we behave.

You should never hate who you are; you should hate what society tells you to be. Society has created you; maturity is creating yourself.

In the concentration camp, we fear the guards; in the totalitarian regime, we fear the government; in the free world, we fear the people we know, the people we love.

We exist, we expose ourselves to the herd, they then interpret us, this creates anxiety. Unfortunately, I see no end to this schism because people must in the current economic system expose their identity to the herd because they need to work.

Our greatest hopes and worst fears lie in being labelled. How people interpret us has a huge bearing on how happy we are.

Many people remark about how they would hate to be famous. To have that level of scrutiny within your life would be nothing short of suicide. Now you must apply that same fear and apprehension to the non-famous or normal individual. In this case, you fear the people who know you. You fear your friends; they mould you. You fear your co-workers; they shape you. You fear the people you recognise when you walk down the street; they decide you. If we were famous, we would acknowledge the anxiety consciously. With the normal person, this anxiety is unconscious.

There is a conflict raging in the minds of men: The system says expose yourself, but this exposure means one can become adversely labelled. This is the Labelling Conflict.

Life is often a battle between desire and being labelled.

Desire vs labelling. We desire sex but can be negatively labelled as a result. We desire money but can be negatively labelled through work problems.

The Labelling Conflict: You desire things in life, but this desire exposes you to interpretation from the individual or herd. You need sexual fulfilment but become subordinate to the person you have sexual relations with. You need money to survive but become a slave to how your co-workers interpret you.

Labelling Conflict: Men and women to a degree are so afraid of being labelled negatively. For instance, they are afraid of being labelled a "virgin." That causes them to seek sex, and they can become adversely labelled as a result.

Often, the pendulum swings between desire and labelling. We desire sex or money or something else, but if obtained wrongly, we get negatively labelled.

We want to live but this living often conflicts with interpretation.

People's behaviour on anonymous forums on the internet differs from their behaviour in the real world. Why is this? It is because in the real world they are exposing their full identity to the observing herd and this manipulates how they behave.

All the conforming class have is their interpretation, but it stings like no other.

We are in a bind. We need for various reasons to interact with others, but this interaction can expose us to negative labelling. We need to work to earn money, but by doing so we can be treated negatively by other co-workers or the boss. Society is in a catch-22. We need interaction as humans, but this very interaction can result in negative labelling.

Labelling Bind. You meet friends, they invite you out and because you don't wish to offend them, you agree. This "going out" then exposes you to more and more people, which you come to fear, which in turn can expose you to even more people. This is the Labelling Chain Reaction. It is a chain reaction. You are afraid of a negative label, which dictates your behaviour, which in turn leads you to be labelled even more.

Labelling Chain Reaction: Think of the nuclear fission chain reaction. One neutron releases two neutrons, those two neutrons release four neutrons and so on. That is what knowing people does. One person that knows you means more people will know you. That you are afraid of being labelled adversely by one person means you become labelled by other people just to pacify (avoid a negative label) the original person who knows you.

Money exposes us to interpretation; desire exposes us to interpretation; then interpretation exposes us to more interpretation.

In the battle between desire, money and interpretation, the outcome is conformity.

My philosophy is flawed in a sense that the economic system conflicts with it. I can suggest that one limits being known in their social life, in order to be more secure. But then one must work to pay bills. This in turn makes us insecure and often leads us into the arms of relationships itself because we are so afraid of the opinions of those we work with. Ergo, it leads to the Labelling Bind.

Imagine you know Person A (PA) in work. (PA) invites you out for drinks on a Friday. You don't actually want to go, but you know (PA) will be disappointed (Labelling Anxiety) in you should you not go. So, you accept his offer. You agree to meet up (Labelling Bind.) When out having a drink (PA) introduces you to another person, Person B (PB). So, you have gone from knowing one person to knowing two. Now, on another day, you are minding your own business doing shopping in the shopping store and you see (PB), who is with his different friend Person C (PC). You stop and chat to (PB) then introduces you to (PC). Now you know three people: (PA),

(PB) and (PC). So the initial fear of being negatively labelled (Labelling Anxiety) by (PA), which in turn made you socialize (Labelling Bind) and has now made you be known by two more people (PB) and (PC) (Labelling Chain Reaction). This is the Labelling Chain Reaction brought on by the Labelling Bind brought on by the Labelling Anxiety.

Desire and money both expose us to labelling, which in turn exposes us to even more labelling via the Labelling Bind and the Labelling Chain Reaction.

The irony of labels is that we fear being labelled a loner or odd and hence socialize with other people and hence become afraid of being negatively labelled by them. The immature individual is in a catch-22. They do not wish to be labelled a social recluse, but they also don't wish to be negatively labelled by another. The urge not to be labelled odd is much greater than the fear of being negatively labelled by someone they know. Thus, they broadcast themselves to the greater population and become controlled. This game haunts them to the day they die.

Threatened With Labels ——— Conforms ——— Becomes Labelled

Fig 2: *Man is condemned to be labelled. We exist and are threatened with being negatively labelled should we not conform (not adhere to the economic system). This is the Labelling Bind. To neutralize this threat, we conform, but in doing so we become labelled and hence controlled.*

A prime example of this is marriage. It is imposed on the individual but then they become subordinate to their partner's interpretation of them and vice versa (The Labelling Anxiety). They then must meet friends and family of their partner (The Labelling Bind), exposing their identity to even more people and thus becoming afraid of being labelled negatively by these other people (Labelling Chain Reaction). So basically, the individual is caught either way. They live in solitude and thus become negatively labelled or they conform in which case they are fearful of a negative label and sometimes actually become negatively labelled. The marriage could fail, or they could lose friends in which the positive adoration morphs into negative opinion.

Social media is a prime example of the Labelling Bind and Labelling Chain Reaction. If we choose not to be on social media, we get negatively labelled and thus this threat motivates us to be on social media to avoid a negative label. The Labelling Anxiety makes us fear being labelled negatively, so we go on social media to be part of the crowd (The Labelling Bind). But in being on social media, we get labelled anyway as we expose our identity to even more people and must behave a certain way in order to be approved (The Labelling Chain Reaction).

The Labelling Anxiety and Labelling Bind: Imagine a friend asks you to meet for coffee. You say no because you are busy. That same friend asks you one month later the same question, to meet for coffee. Again, you say no for a certain reason. The same friend asks you again, a month later, to meet for coffee. Now you are thinking that if you reject them again, they will be disappointed in you (negatively label you). So now, at the third time of asking you meet up. The threat of a negative label (Labelling Anxiety) has decided how you behave (Labelling Bind.)

The Labelling Bind demonstrates the anxiety with being known. A friend or perhaps a partner asks you to do something you do not wish to do. But you end up doing it anyway, despite your reluctance because you know that if you do not do it, you will be labelled negatively by the said friend or partner. The moral is as Schopenhauer alluded to that being known leads to angst. So if you minimize being known (as hard as it is to do in the present world) you can become happier in person.

The positives of labelling are morality and compassion. The negatives are insecurity and narcissism.

There exists a bind. We are afraid of being negatively labelled should we not socialize and then we again are afraid of being negatively labelled when as a result of socializing. Take a young woman. She is afraid of being perceived as odd should she live in solitude away from everyone. So she exposes her identity to society (socializes) and again becomes afraid of how she is labelled. To neutralize the anxiety associated with this exposure, she conforms to what we generally expect women to be. The same can be applied to men.

The Labelling Anxiety gives birth to the Labelling Bind, which gives birth to the Labelling Chain Reaction, which gives birth to the Labelling Anxiety and Labelling Bind again.

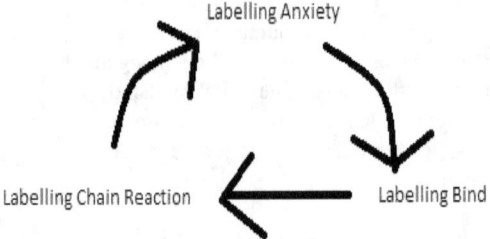

Labelling Anxiety

Labelling Chain Reaction   Labelling Bind

Fig 3: *The Labelling Anxiety gives birth to the Labelling Bind, which in turn gives birth to the Labelling Chain Reaction and so the cycle continues.*

Being known is a psychological rape upon our identity. But in a world wherein socialization is seen as the norm, our minds must adapt to take this existential onslaught. They do so through conforming. By conforming one can socialize and be secure in knowing that they will be labelled correctly.

You are not afraid of being laughed at by a dog or a cat. But you are afraid of being laughed at by another human being. You are not afraid of a negative label from a dog or a cat. But you are afraid of a negative label from another human being. Being known by a human is vastly different from being known by any other animal. So how do we negate this fear of being laughed at by other humans? Simple, we conform. And it is this labelling mechanism, which I theorize is defective in those with schizophrenia.

Once known, man is stalked, incarcerated, condemned and existentially guillotined. It is most dangerous to be known.

People are more likely when on anonymous forums to be rude or condescending. Whereas in real life they would not behave as such. What that says is that when we are known, we tend to adjust our behaviour so as to be positively labelled.

We are slaves to money, desire and interpretation. Unconsciously these three things are deciding our behaviour. Imagine you are at work and get the urge to buy a cup of coffee. First is the desire to have it, that motivates you. Then you must check you have enough money to buy it. In order to have money you must work for it. Then you must get permission to leave your workplace to buy it. You must be positively interpreted by your boss or co-workers.

Labelling is the glue that binds society together.

We are controlled by money, desire and interpretation. Money is economics; desire is evolutionary; interpretation is sociological. The system requires that we work; then we need to eat and have sex; finally, we become a slave to those who know us.

We cannot see the oppression. We cannot see the bind of being known. If we err in life the neighbours will not like us. Likewise, if we walk by our neighbours without saying hello, they will not like us either.

Work backwards from the criminals and the escorts and the latent homosexuals. They fear being reported on. They fear being known. They know they will not be approved. Now analyse mainstream society. They have no anxiety or trepidation in exposing their identity to the herd. But the society is still there, analysing ruthlessly. Thus, they instead live for society's approval and endorsement. When you expose your full identity to society, seeking approval becomes a by-product. Few realize this and even fewer can defy it.

The insecure suffer an intense Labelling Anxiety.

Society mistakes being labelled positively for not being labelled at all.

Being known promotes social control. Interpretation (labelling) controls society.

You cannot understand schizophrenia without understanding the Labelling Phenomenon.

The labelling mechanism that controls society and makes them conform is malfunctioning in the schizophrenic individual. The Labelling Anxiety makes the common individual conform; it makes the schizophrenic delusional.

We only worry about violence from another person when faced with it. In contrast, we unconsciously fear being labelled by society every second of every day of every year. This is the ultimate fear of mankind: Being labelled by another person or persons. So how do we compensate for this dilemma?

We do so through conforming. Conformity becomes the means by which we can advertise our identity to the greater world whilst at the same time be secure in knowing that we will be labelled positively by the world.

If you take two people who meet each other by chance on the city street. Both must acknowledge each other (say hello) in order to be approved by each other. There exists a sort of game theory conflict between both. Now you could apply this to two (or more) people who do not know each other but interact, such as walking by each other on a city street.

Person A

Person B		Does not say hello	Says hello
	Does not say hello	x	x
	Says hello	x	0

Fig 4: *Conflict (a negative label) arises on three occasions. Only when the two people both behave positively to each other, is conflict avoided.*

Being known is psychological assault upon our identity. That is why we react in a certain way to people we know. That is why we say "hello" to someone we meet out and about. Why not walk past them without acknowledging them?

Interaction between humans blinds us to the universe. We are distracted from the true realities of the world through the very fact that we socialize with each other. We are so consumed with how we are labelled that we negate the atom and the miracle of the universe

Everything is being interpreted. Every interaction is being scrutinized. Every time you meet someone be it ordering a cup of coffee or talking to a friend, your unconscious mind is making decisions. "Is that appropriate or inappropriate?" "Is it acceptable or unacceptable?"

If we were all blind, life paradoxically, would be much simpler. We would not be worried by what people thought of us. We would not fear their labels.

You will not value your anonymity in life unless you err.

Think of two people who work together. When they meet in the street or in the office in the morning, they greet each other. Now look at what happens when one person does not greet the other. They fall out. Essentially everyone's behaviour is controlled by the other individual. This behaviour of greeting people is decided by the fact that they know each other. Another way to think of it is that imagine these people had never known each other and let us say they pass by each other on a busy city street. They just walk by each other and never see each other again. That they do not know each other means they cannot be controlled by each other. What I am trying to convey is that one's behaviour is decided by the people who know you. Society decides society.

We are born free. Then parents label us. Then we are educated and labelled by our friends. We then must work and become labelled by our co-workers. These three entities (parents; friends; co-workers) all determine our wills and wants purely because they can label us.

Despite all the crime no one thinks to ban interaction altogether to prevent crime. If you don't interact with society, you cannot be a criminal.

The unconscious fear is shielded by the essentiality of conformity. The unconscious fear is the Labelling Anxiety which masquerades as conformity.

The Labelling Anxiety is like dark matter. We cannot perceive it but it dictates our behaviour.

The reality is that you are a "good person" because you are deeply afraid.

This Labelling Anxiety component of your psyche is in relentless operation. When you chat to the barista in the coffee shop, it is in work. "Do this and do that; don't do this and don't do that."

Labelling Anxiety: Imagine an individual gets invited out for a few drinks to a bar wherein they will meet other people. Immediately the mind of such a person goes into a state of panic. Their Labelling Anxiety kicks in. They are going to be meeting people and as such will be labelled by those people. So how does the mind of this individual invalidate this apprehension or fear. It does so through conforming because the unconscious mind recognises that through conforming, they will be labelled positively by that group of people. So, the individual in question dresses in nice clothes, does their hair, puts on their make-up etc. Now this Labelling Anxiety only exists for a fraction of a second before their mind neutralizes it through the thought of conforming. But an anxiety that exists for only a fraction of a second still exists.

People are a mirror into our souls. What they think of us as they look at us determines how we feel.

We adjust our behaviour when known face to face. The proof can be seen by when people use anonymous internet forum accounts. They behave in a way in which they would not if their full identity were known. Give a man a mask, as they say. Goffman was dead right. We are actors, trying at all times, to be approved and labelled correctly.

If you do not have an identity, you cannot be attacked; if you don't exist, you cannot be psychologically raped.

What you cannot see, is that when you expose yourself to other people, you become afraid of what they think of you.

The Bandwagon Effect: That everyone else is doing it, so must you to avoid being laughed at.

The genius is lauded, the serial killer vilified, but both once known are controlled by the prying eyes of society.

I remember reading about a man who was on disability for his bad hearing. He said that his mother, although not narcissistic, was putting him under pressure to get a job and have friends. Now analyse why she was doing this. She was doing it because she wanted her son to fall under the correct labels. In other words, she was afraid of how he was interpreted. She associated those who did not work and who had no friends, as being eccentric delinquents. When people asked her, what was her son doing, she was embarrassed by having to tell these people that he was doing nothing. Again, she was governed by labels and she was not even a full-blown narcissist.

"Stigma is a process whereby the reaction of others spoils normal identity." - Erving Goffman. We are all stigmatised and the net result of this stigmatization is conformity.

The ideal human is a social construct.

Social media spawn's narcissism within people. They unconsciously calculate that because they are distributing their identity publicly, they have to conform in order to be approved. So, they become obsessed with self-image and hence narcissistic traits take over their conscience.

"We are all just actors trying to control and manage our public image, we act based on how others might see us." - Erving Goffman. We behave in a way that enables us to be positively labelled. To add to this, we then pretend to be happy because this is how the system tells us to be happy. The insecure (and often narcissistic) individual then says: "I look happy; therefore, I must be happy." This is Pretence Happiness. But is one actually happy?

"I am supposed to enjoy it, therefore I must be enjoying it." This is Pretence Happiness.

How we conduct ourselves is a fabrication. It is illusory. It is all a response to being known. We are shaped by the economic system. The stereotypical man or woman is a fashion, a role that people play. "Most people are other people. Their thoughts are someone else's opinions, their lives a mimicry, their passions a quotation." - Oscar Wilde.

The Marxists wonder why capitalism has not been eradicated. Three huge components in why it prevails are A) You make the middle class fear each other. You expose them to the herd when young and they come to fear the interpretation of the said herd. This motivates them to conform. They are also very afraid to step out of line. B) You brainwash the middle class on Pretence Happiness. You tell them they can procure happiness by accumulating X, Y and Z. By getting married, having children, owning a house, a car, going on two holidays a year, buying the latest clothes and gadgets, that you can become happy. This is a material or narcissistic happiness. "If you don't do this, you will not experience life to the fullest," says the system. C) You give them just enough money to be able to afford this Pretence Happiness. Not too much, just enough.

It is a concentration camp without barbed wire. The middle class think they are living life to the fullest by conforming. All they are doing is contributing to the wealth of the bourgeoise. That is their main purpose. But they hold the power (the middle class). They can if they were not so impressionable, rebel and demand a bigger slice of the cake. But again, it comes back to how happy they determine themselves to be. They are prepared to settle for such a small chunk of the profits because we brainwash them to.

The enemies of the middle class are the middle class themselves because through the threat of labelling, they enforce conformity. The person who deviates gets negatively labelled. This threat and the threat of not living life to the fullest makes them conform. The enemy is not the Bourgeoise for they only reap the benefits of macro scale conformity. The enemy is the middle class themselves, that regulate each other through labelling.

It is only when the middle class are not content, that they seek change. Deprive them enough and they rebel. You keep society obedient by keeping them happy.

Is it the carrot or the stick, with regards the middle class? It is both. You make them afraid through labelling, that being the odd one out means they will be demeaned. That is the stick. The carrot is you implant in their minds the illusion of living the dream life, where they are above all else happy. Then you just give them enough money to procure this dream life.

The middle class through education and parenthood, regulates itself.

Animals only fear each other physically, not psychologically. Another cat is not afraid of being laughed at or demeaned by another cat. With humans, we fear other humans both physically and psychologically. We are afraid of a negative interpretation from those who know us. This terror of being labelled haunts us.

They say fame is fickle. The reality is that it is interpretation that is fickle. You just cannot depend on people to positively endorse you.

You are not afraid of what your dog thinks of you, but you are afraid of what your friend thinks of you.

There are two states: One, the world of people you know and who know you. Two, the world of people you don't know and who don't know you. Anonymity is as vital as friendship for a healthy mind. When you are too known, it can cause problems.

Fame and criminality are the two extremes of being known. Both are unhealthy.

Man is the only animal that is afraid of being laughed at and this fear has a huge bearing on how he behaves. Being known is a perversion.

The price of existence as a human is being known. David Foster Wallace gave a great example of what motivates people to commit suicide. He used the analogy of a skyscraper in flames and the only option is to choose a less torturous method of death by leaping from the said skyscraper. With regards suicide of people who are clinically depressed I would wager a large reason for many suicides (but not all) was being labelled. They did something and were labelled negatively, and this pushes them over the edge. The torture of being labelled is much greater than the pain of suicide. There is so much anxiety associated with being labelled and man is the only animal that is afflicted by this threat.

Through exposure we slowly strangle each other; if death does not kill you, life surely will.

We need to label to police the system. To make it functional.

Being looked at by another person is the same as looking into the mirror. And looking in the mirror is the same as being looked at by another person. Often the mirror is our greatest foe.

If you think of the famous person, they must live a very precision engineered life. Why? They do so because their identity is exposed to the world, who then threaten them with labels, should they choose to deviate from this precision engineered life. Now you must apply this same mechanism to the non-famous individual, as in you. Who threatens you through labelling? Who are you afraid of? You are afraid of your parents, your friends, your neighbours, your co-workers etc.

Imagine someone you know assaults you physically. You would interpret that person negatively. Now imagine you are walking down the city street and they walk past you without saying hello. You would also interpret that person negatively. So, if you interpret both situations regarding this person negatively, it can be assumed that them knowing you, is violence upon your identity.

Camus once mentioned that the only way to deal with an unfree world is through an act of rebellion. Unfortunately, there is only so much behaviour that is tolerated with the current system. The individual can only rebel so much before they are negatively labelled by society.

Because of labelling, society is finely tuned. You can do A, B and C; you cannot do X, Y and Z. The society you see before you is a response to labelling.

What precedes conformity/capitalistic insecurity is the Labelling Anxiety; what precedes the Labelling Anxiety is being known; what precedes being known is existence as a human being.

Sartre said we are condemned to choose but we are also condemned to be labelled, despite doing nothing and our choices are severely influenced by the fact that we will be labelled.

Your Labelling Anxiety says: I need a partner; overcoming your Labelling Anxiety says: I can be happy alone. Your Labelling Anxiety says: I need a good job; overcoming your Labelling Anxiety says: I can work in any job. Your Labelling Anxiety says: I need to be good looking; overcoming your Labelling Anxiety says: I am not dependent on appearance to be happy.

The Labelling Anxiety makes you insecure and makes you desperate. As a result of the Labelling Anxiety the two most common words in your unconscious mind are: I need. I need a partner; I need a good job; I need to look good; I need to be popular etc. And because you keep saying "I need," you approach each day in uncertain terms. Essentially you become an agent of gratification wherein when what you need or wish for materializes, you feel good or gratified. But this gratification erodes into the night sky and you wake up anxious the next morning because you again need to hit targets in order to become happy (gratified). When you tackle your unconscious Labelling Anxiety you can rewire your brain to convey gratitude.

Evolutionary psychologists assert that the male and female differ regarding procreation. The male has multiple partners; the female carefully selects her partner. I do not disagree with that. But with humans one must also factor in labelling. Both men and women must be careful with how they are labelled by society with regards to sex. Men can be classified as "perverts" and women can be classified as "whores." This threat of a negative label directs them towards marriage because they are not labelled negatively when they have sex when married.

The ontologically secure individual cannot perceive the effects of labelling.

People have a habit of blaming the powerful institutions such as the government, the army, the prison system, the psychiatric institutions and so on. But one must also blame society itself. Society is one of those powerful entities. The average man with short hair, dressed a certain way, living in a certain house, driving a certain car, behaving a certain way, is not motivated by appeasing the government or the army or the doctors; he is motivated in pleasing his peers. It is his partner, parents, his friends, his co-workers and so on, that decide him. Society in a Darwinian method shapes society itself through exposing the individuals in society to each other.

If you take the flight or fight with regards the Labelling Anxiety. You can either flee the anxiety through not being known or you fight it through conforming.

Man is the only animal that can be a genius or a criminal.

Fame kills; fame does kill. Fame is just a variation of criminality, albeit not as interesting.

There exists a bind. The economic system promotes interaction, but we then become subservient to the interpretation of those we interact with.

Are we patrons of conformity or victims?

In the concentration camp we commonly call life, interpretation is the barbed wire.

Our actions determine our labels. Even if you do nothing, you still get labelled.

The tragedy for western society is that they are so sure they have not been manipulated and this is one of the triumphs of capitalism.

Social media is bringing Franz Kafka's The Trial to life. Being known is violence because you become a slave to one's interpretation of you. What social media does is magnify this violence.

The most damning indictment of the current system is that even though we do not freeze or starve, we are still anxious. Forget about our genius to predict the atom or our artistic merit, society still currently is drenched with anxiety. We talk about eradicating disease and preventing climate change and they are necessary things to do. But one other thing we must do is eliminate anxiety as well.

Success is not without its demons.

The conformist and the schizophrenic are both troubled by the same anxiety (Labelling Anxiety). But their retrospective unconscious minds respond to it differently.

Franz Kafka's The Trial is indicative of the power of being known. Imagine you are a conventional individual minding your own business and keeping within the law, that is suddenly arrested for an unknown crime and paraded before the public. Your identity will go from being resolute in not being known to being terrified of this new label which is the result of being known. You will despair at how society now perceives you. Therefore I remark, that to be known in this world is to commit existential suicide because once known you are labelled and once labelled you are controlled.

Opinion makes life unbearable.

To be known and to be labelled are the two sides of the same coin. You cannot be known if you are not labelled and you cannot be labelled if you are not known. If you are not labelled it means you are not known and likewise if you are not known, you cannot be labelled. The consequence of being known is that you are labelled and if you are labelled it is understood that you have become known.

We are in effect psychologically violating people through labelling them.

We live in a world of continuous threats. People are bombarding the individual with threats through labelling them. The world as we know it is in part a response to this bombardment of labels. We regulate society not just through money but also through interpretation.

We are condemned to exist, then condemned to choose, then condemned to be known, then condemned to be labelled and finally then condemned to despair.

Dying isn't the worst thing in life; being known is.

Think back to when you were an adolescent. You were consumed by image. You needed the correct clothes, the correct haircut, the correct everything etc. You needed these things because you wanted to fit in with the crowd. You did not want them to laugh at you. Your mind becomes programmed on desire to be happy and hence you became an agent of gratification. You then simply carry this mentality into adulthood wherein you need the correct life. Maturity is eroding this diseased mentality.

We can only label because we can use language. Labelling is a product of language.

Paradox of exposure: We need company and yet we fear it also.

If you think of the Labelling Anxiety with respect to some infamous criminal such as Pablo Escobar, who was a Colombian cartel boss. In order for him to accumulate his wealth and power he must expose himself to people. These people include rival bosses, people of authority such as army personnel, lieutenants who might want to take his position and so on. These people make his life troublesome. That he has exposed himself to these people, he comes to fear them. What is the reverse? The reverse is that he retreats to solitude on some mountain and lives off the land. But he has no wealth in such a position. Now you must apply this to the average law-abiding citizen. In order to make money and own a house, they must expose their identity to people, and they come to fear the interpretation of these said people. They can choose to negate this anxiety by living on welfare but will possess a poor standard of living.

Man is the only insecure animal in existence.

To remark that everyone is a threat is not paranoid. It is existential. Everyone who knows you is another person who can condemn you and hence control you. You can only truly be free in anonymity.

Interaction is the source of all our woes. No interaction equals no crime.

The female's obsession with beauty is a direct response to being known by men. Likewise, the male's obsession with money or success is a direct response to being known by women.

Anonymity is one of life's little-known pleasures.

Every day is a battle to be labelled correctly.

Once we label someone, we remember them.

We are constrained by money or capital. That is obvious. Other obvious ones are desire or will, as Schopenhauer called it. Religion is another huge constraint within society. But the one other thing that also influences how we behave is interpretation. How people label us dictates our behaviour also.

The minimalists should apply their philosophy to people and not just possessions.

The wild animal may worry about food or predators, but they never worry about being liked. That is solely a trait of the animal that can speak.

If fame is horrible, then so is being known, because fame is just the extreme end of being known.

When we are walking down the street, we are not afraid of being attacked. But what we are afraid of is being humiliated or laughed at. And that is around people we don't even know. What of this fear around the people we do know?

We take existence for granted when we feel melancholic because we are not liked.

If you want to be genuinely happy: Live alone in solitude. But are you prepared to defy the herd that imposes people on you? "A man can be himself only so long as he is alone; and if he does not love solitude, he will not love freedom; for it is only when he is alone that he is really free." - Arthur Schopenhauer.

I said in previous notes: "Trust is the source of our woe." I was wrong because before trust comes interaction. You must interact with someone to trust them. Therefore, interaction is the source of all our woe. Interaction makes us insecure.

The herd are ruthless and merciless. Any man or woman who decides to deviate from the path of marriage and family is labelled fittingly. This fear haunts the conscience of the young naïve individual. Faced with the threat of being an individual and being labelled a heretic, such an individual conforms implicitly to appease the tribe.

There is a pattern immerging with reality television stars, in that a good number of them commit suicide after exposure. They do so because they have become labelled.

The man who goes alone is often seen as the alpha male; the woman who goes alone is treated as a leper.

We are condemning ourselves through psychological rape masquerading as friendship. The people we know decide so much of us. They attack our identity. They destroy us.

People will wonder what I mean by saying we fear being known. Narcissism by default is the fear of being known, the fear of being labelled. That is why narcissists are extremely status conscious. But think of the individual who has plastic surgery or spends an hour in the gym or obsesses over buying the latest clothes or gadgets, they do all those things to be approved, by other people, but also by themselves. In other words, they fear being laughed at and hence fear being known.

When you sit in Starbucks drinking your latte and minding your own business, you may not know the other people in the place, but you are interacting with them. You are always labelling their behaviour and they are labelling yours.

We are all Instagram models without the fame. We depend on partners, friends, co-workers to approve of us.

We have been so inured from a young age with regards meeting people and socialization that we don't sense the threats. We cannot detect the fear that accompanies being known. We respond to it unconsciously though.

With animals there is no psychological threat. A kangaroo is not afraid of being laughed at or demeaned by another kangaroo. Humans are afraid of being laughed at and demeaned by other humans. Knowing other people as a human is psychological violence upon our conscience. How your mind responds to this threat leads to conformity, leads to narcissism and I suspect (but I could be wrong) leads to schizophrenia.

There is such a problem with sexual crime and yet they will not ban sexual interaction outright. They won't do that because they (the powers that be) recognise that in this concentration camp we call life, people need to have sex, to start families and give birth to the next generation who will contribute to the economic system. It may sound extreme but if you ban interaction completely, in other words make no one be within ten yards of each other, you will remove a lot of crime from present day life. But can such a world ever be envisaged, let alone fabricated? Part of the problem is that we are so inured on normal life, that all other worlds are forsaken.

It is interaction that makes sinners and victims out of all of us.

If you take someone who works in a professional environment, male or female, they have a certain dress code they must adhere to. Ask yourself, why don't they come into work dressed in shorts and a t-shirt? They don't because they know they will be negatively labelled by co-workers and their boss. The threat of being negatively labelled has influenced their behaviour. Labelling is a means of social control.

You can't erase your identity from the minds of people that know you. Once they know you and you them, your fate is decided. This is how the herd promotes conformity.

Imagine you went viral tomorrow. Apply that same degree of apprehension to your life as you know it now.

The individual conceives that when people positively label them, they will become happy. But this is why they do not become happy because not everyone positively labels them. In the end they get slaughtered by their own craving for likeability. The trick is to overcome this narcissism and limit being known. Take for instance a social media blogger. That they are exposing their identity to the herd, they conceive that they need to look well. But after a while the audience gets bored or even negatively labels them, so the individual in question tries to become more beautiful in order to receive applause. They might have plastic surgery or spend a fortune on new clothes or starve themselves for a new body shape. But this mechanism is not enjoyment or happiness; it is suffering; it is being at the mercy of the interpretation of whomever labels you. Now I see no end in sight for this mechanism, because the current economic system necessitates that we expose our identity to society in order to make money to have a standard of living.

The Hedgehogs Dilemma can be applied to labelling. You interact with people, you risk being labelled negatively by them. You avoid them completely and you suffer because you are human, all too human.

That we have parents and are educated we learn not to see people as threats. Instead we are taught to have friends, to get to know people, to socialize. But these things only increase our angst because we become subordinate to the opinions of others, of the tribe.

Shame is a masterful influencer.

We are effectively socialized against our will when young and then we become forever known by our peers and forever condemned by them. Imagine for instance you get invited to a wedding by a close friend and you do not go. Now the friend thinks that is rude and falls out with you over it. You then are attacked by guilt and remorse. Now imagine you had never known this person. There would be no guilt over them. What this says is that the people we know control our behaviour. They determine how we feel about ourselves. A large portion of our lives is spent trying to make people like us or maintain the fact that they like us.

Our actions determine our labels and the threat of being labelled determines our actions.

You cannot fall out with friends if you have no friends.

Conformity and labels are linked. In conforming you become labelled; being potentially labelled endeavours to implore you to conform. So, if conformity is linked to labelling and labelling is linked to schizophrenia, then conformity is linked to schizophrenia. I believe the brainwashing to conform when young has a bearing on the disease.

"Our existence precedes our essence," said Sartre and in vying for purpose we adopt conformity and in doing so become labelled. Our essence precedes being labelled. In our hunt for purpose we invite demons. We make ourselves but in making ourselves we label ourselves.

Existence ——— Essence ——— Labelled

Fig 5: *Bear in mind that once man exists, he is condemned to be labelled. He cannot not be labelled. Even if he does nothing, he becomes labelled (A loner; eccentric; strange etc.)*

The price of existence is choice and the price of choice is being labelled. Even the man who does nothing does something.

Fame is the most repugnant form of being approved.

We try to give up gambling or smoking or drinking but never interaction. Interaction is seen as something we must do.

Interaction is the source of so many problems with the individual. If you can learn to live without it, you can be so much more assured in your existence.

Interaction is like a game of craps. We try to roll the dice in our favour. We want people to behave as we wish, but they don't always do so. This failure leads to angst.

Normative Social Influence is a type of social influence leading to conformity. It is defined in social psychology as "the influence of other people that leads us to conform in order to be liked and accepted by them." In other words, we try to be positively labelled by other people and we achieve this by conforming.

You would think that the riches of capitalism would make us happier, when in fact they make us unhappier. Why is this? One of the reasons, as Durkheim may remark, is that we put severe pressure on ourselves in response to the threat of being labelled. What I mean by this is that we see what other people have and A) either try to mimic them or B) try to outcompete them. We are exposed to people and we instinctively think that if I just obtain X, Y and Z, then I will impress these people and hence will feel good about myself. The person is perpetually saying "I need." "I need to date that person," which means "I need to be seen with that person." "I need to buy that car or dress," which means "I need to be seen driving that car or be seen wearing that dress." It is hard to explain, but the greater the quality of life, it seems the more desperate people become to accrue adoration. Approbation becomes the currency of happiness. But when you rewind back all the dominos, one of the first dominos to fall is socialization. We expose children to each other, and they then come to fear each other. You then teach them that being a grateful loner is wrong and you will be laughed at if you do that. The fear of being laughed at, otherwise known as being negatively labelled, has a huge influence in how they behave.

Education

"Children must be taught how to think, not what to think." - Margaret Mead.

A lot of people do not enjoy school and yet it is mandatory. When things in life are mandatory, they are mandatory for a reason. School as it turns out (along with parenthood) is where our young brains are manipulated to operate a certain way. That is why education is necessary. The powers that be want to control society through education and they succeed. Society then becomes obsessed with certain things like image, sex, conversation, work etc.

With education, the mind becomes a slave to labelling. We learn that making others happy for us, makes us in turn feel good. This (along with parents) is where the herd mentality is enforced upon us. We become subordinate to the tribe because of education and hence subordinate to labelling.

That we are thrown in the snake-pit of education when young shapes our impressionable conscience. We instinctively learn that in order to endorse ourselves, we must be endorsed by our fellow classmates; in order to approve of ourselves, we must be approved by our fellow classmates. So how does this young individual procure endorsement and approval? They conform. In other words, the young men have money and status and the young women look attractive. They then transfer this sick, revolting and toxic attitude into adulthood and that is why they are so insecure.

The mature, in order to survive, conform; the immature, in order to survive, adopt narcissistic traits.

Genius I believe is borne out of a defiance of education.

Those in Soviet Russia led a revolt against communism. It strangled their freedom and oppressed them. It told them how to live and how to behave. The exact same principle applies to education except we never rebel against how we were educated. We are so brainwashed that we don't even realize who we are and what we have become as adults.

Education is indoctrination. Education conditions us to become addicts of conformity. Just as we have scientific models that explain the universe, we have models that describe how to live. Conformity is one such model.

When I was young, I kept asking why I had to go to school. When I grew up, I kept asking the same thing under a different tone. Why is education enforced?

Why are we so anxious to trust others? Why are we so desperate to be with others? We have been indoctrinated from childhood to believe that we must have others in our lives. We know of no other way to live because we have been bred this way like machines. The Labelling Anxiety is spawned in part through mandatory education.

Education in wealthy countries is a large reason why people are insecure. They grow up not to be compassionate to each other but to out-compete each other.

Education is mandatory because it prepares you for life. It teaches us to conform. It makes you dependent on others (friendship) to derive pleasure from life.

Because of education man is implored to live a life of conformity. He is so because he becomes afraid of being negatively labelled by his peers and because of this he comes to see life as marriage and work.

"Ideally, what should be said to every child, repeatedly, throughout his or her school life is something like this: 'You are in the process of being indoctrinated. We have not yet evolved a system of education that is not a system of indoctrination. We are sorry, but it is the best we can do. What you are being taught here is an amalgam of current prejudice and the choices of this particular culture. The slightest look at history will show how impermanent these must be. You are being taught by people who have been able to accommodate themselves to a regime of thought laid down by their predecessors. It is a self-perpetuating system. Those of you who are more robust and individual than others will be encouraged to leave and find ways of educating yourself — educating your own judgements. Those that stay must remember, always, and all the time, that they are being moulded and patterned to fit into the narrow and particular needs of this particular society." - Doris Lessing.

The saddest part of life is that we dare not question it. We never ask: Why am I doing what I do? We simply accept the path that is laid out for us without even the faintest reprimand within our forlorn souls.

Education is a snake-pit. We expose young children to the herd, and they become insecure because of it.

Education teaches them to become reliant on each other. It tutors them to work for reward. It disciplines them to think alike rather than critically think as an individual.

The only education of substance is where the individual educates themselves.

Natural curiosity is the finest educator of all.

99% of people on this planet are machines and will not achieve anything of note in their existence. They will just get up for work, work and come home and go to sleep.

We are machines that are simply coded psychologically to behave the same way, to achieve the same goals, to suffer the same mistakes. We are all the same.

We are all identical because the education tyranny has deprived us of the ability to critically think.

Parents really are just tools of the economic system; they teach their children to become parents themselves.

We become the soldiers of conformity who heed to the commands of the general and die ingloriously in battle and become wasted in the sands of time.

The most important element of education is not learning to read and write or to count or even to enjoy oneself. No, the most important element of this childhood indoctrination is socialization and because of it the next generation grow up to all desire the same things in life of which economies on a macro scale benefit. They become inured on fellow people and hence afraid of them through this systematic brainwashing and the result is we get marriages and work and many other qualities. It is not coincidental that the masses all unconsciously covet the same trades. They do so only because they are programmed to do so and not by their own willingness. Education despite what one thinks is what controls the masses.

"The illiterate of the 21st century will not be those who cannot read and write, but those who cannot learn, unlearn, and relearn." - Alvin Toffler.

To control the people, educate them; to give power to the individual, let him educate himself.

Find your own voice before you grow old and lose it altogether. You achieve far more in life by being who you are and never letting others choose who you are. Own yourself above all else.

We are blessed with freedom in the west and yet when we gain it, we imprison ourselves through work and marriage.

The system we have chosen is an economic one.

Margaret Atwood was outraged when her book The Handmaids Tale was determined to be the work of masterful science fiction. She was right to be angry. The Handmaids Tale is not science fiction or even fiction; it is what is happening right now.

That we are free in this capitalist forest does not mean that we cannot be brainwashed. We are suffocated by the invisible walls of conformity. Our liberation is precisely the school of our brainwashing.

Education is indoctrination; it is a means to conquer society.

Society creates all and society executes all.

I cannot emphasize it enough. The reason you instinctively think of family is because that is how you have been taught by the system and that has been done from an incredibly young age.

That the individual is so brainwashed, they do not see the economic system telling, educating and teaching them on how to behave. To the naïve individual, the way you behave is simply the way you behave as a human to become happy. The truth is the economic system has told you how to behave in a method that benefits the economic system.

The worst way to learn things is to learn them by being taught by someone else. The best way to learn things is to teach yourself. Let your curiosity do the teaching.

The most important component of education is not the teachers teaching the children; it is the children teaching each other.

Educations success is in creating a humane society; educations failure is in creating an insecure humane society.

Foucault alludes to power as a factor in shaping our mentality. I would add to that, that those in powerful positions, expose us to each other through education and work and then let us govern each other, at least in the supposedly free countries. In western countries, it is society itself that is the authoritarian dictator.

The greatest failure of education with respect to the male and female of society is that it convinces them that they can only be happy when they are desired. As such this immature and insecure individual matures with the mentality that he or she must be loved in order to be complete.

They do not teach in schools the absurdness of life. They do not tell you that you are an animal composed of trillions of atoms, inhabiting a planet that revolves around a star. This is where the indoctrination starts. This (and through parenthood) is where the Economic Narcissism is instilled in the individual. They want you to be obsessed with work. They want you to be obsessed with sex. They do not even teach psychology in schools because they don't want you to understand yourself. They want you to live on instinct and what is your instinct? To conform.

A problem with the immature of society is that they are still in the educational phase of life in that they try to accrue approval. They dress nice to gain approval; they argue to gain approval; they work to gain approval. The existentially liberated person does not engage in this behaviour. They are simply happy to be alive.

The amount of men and especially women who say to themselves: "If I don't get married, I am missing out in life." You think like this because they have taught you to think like this. Thus, in order to mature in an existential method, one must overcome the twenty odd years of abuse by parents and education.

It is not just what we teach but also how we teach.

We educate society on what is criminal; we also educate them on what dreams they should have.

Education can only do so much. It teaches us how to count, to speak, to make money, to be happy, to behave, to conform. The curious individual, the one who goes far in life, sees what education has done for them and goes further. They start to educate themselves and that is the point that must be reached by everyone.

Michel Foucault: "Schools serve the same social functions as prisons and mental institutions- to define, classify, control, and regulate people."

Education has the same effect on us as social media does, except it implements this effect to us when we are young. People on social media, live for "likes" which is another way of saying they live for endorsement. When people like them, they like themselves. Education does the same thing to us as children, in that we instinctively learn that happiness is making our classmates be impressed by us. Then we just carry this narcissistic attitude into adulthood and conformity is in part a by-product of this. Ok, it is not all bad. The collectivised education of children does produce a compassionate society. But a huge negative is insecurity.

The systematic education of us can only take the individual so far. True wisdom, true freedom lies going further. One in a sense reaches a point wherein they must start to educate themselves to the reality of this universe. That is the point when you become existentially free; that is the point of no return.

Those who remain mediocre in life are those who proclaim that because they are educated, they are smart. It is those who have the hunger and curiosity to seek more than what the current system of education provides, that are rewarded.

To be existentially free is not to defy your education. It is to enhance it or extend it and you do this by educating yourself. The immature individual does not do this until they are old or perhaps never at all. The systematic education radicalizes their minds on relationships and careers. The mature or existentially free individual recognises this brainwashing and then decides to educate themselves. They take what education has given them and then amplify it with their own education.

This is precisely what Jewish people do and it is why they achieve more. They are educated in the textbook system, yes, but they are then told that true wisdom is to educate yourself. Their school education only takes them so far and then they must travel the rest of the way. They have the hunger and curiosity to seek more, to be more.

"Men are born ignorant, not stupid. They are made stupid by education." - Bertrand Russell.

There is something seriously wrong with the system if one can enjoy such luxury in contrast to the poor of this world and still be unhappy. The capitalist has so much in abundance, but they need more. They need to be liked, to be desired. This manifests itself in the form of work and a relationship. Alas when they fail at these things, so too does their zest for life.

The capitalist system is a particularly good system, but it is not perfect. The lack of appreciation for luxury relative to the poverty of the greater world is the most harrowing failure of it.

Your happiness can be material; it can ebb and flow with the tides of success. Or if you are a truly liberated individual, you can derive it from the way you think.

A most interesting individual in society is one that is not liked by the herd.

In order to mature you must counter twenty years of narcissism in parenthood and education.

The colleges are a business. They are an enterprise. They teach you everything about your chosen subject, but they don't teach students to teach themselves.

Society mistakes a system for living. We are convinced when young that doing X, Y and Z is part and parcel of living. This is false. It is just a system. By doing X, Y and Z we contribute to the system. This is then passed off as "living," to make people buy into it.

Education is just a nicer term for state sponsored brainwashing. There is more delusion on planet earth than there is hydrogen in the universe.

"We've bought into the idea that education is about training and "success", defined monetarily, rather than learning to think critically and to challenge. We should not forget that the true purpose of education is to make minds, not careers. A culture that does not grasp the vital interplay between morality and power, which mistakes management techniques for wisdom, which fails to understand that the measure of a civilization is its compassion, not its speed or ability to consume, condemns itself to death." - Chris Hedges.

Do not get me wrong; education is vital for producing a humane world. But a lot of the insecurities that accompany individuals as they mature stem from education. So, the system is not perfect, but then again, no system is.

It does not take a genius to figure out this system. Most people see it when they grow old. They look back and realize they were to an extent taken advantage of. Wisdom alas is being aware of this when you are young.

One of the problems I see with society is that they need to be told what to do and what to want rather than having the courage and curiosity to find out for themselves. This stems from education. The teacher says that this is what is right, and this is what is wrong, and the students believe him or her.

A skilled teacher teaches students to teach themselves.

Education is not just academia. It is also personal growth and maturity as an animal in this universe.

"Chaos is rejecting all you have learned. Chaos is being yourself." - Emil Cioran.

The world is for everyone; the economic system is not.

Think back to your first education when young. They don't teach you about feminist literature discussing the discrepancies in the system of marriage; they don't teach you about Karl Marx and how the capitalist system is rigged in favour of the rich; they don't teach you about the absurdness of the existential landscape; they don't even tell you that you are being brainwashed. They tell you things that make you a slave.

No one ever stands getting their picture taken on their graduation day and says, "You know what, I have been brainwashed the last twenty years by both parents and education." They just cannot see it.

The average person learns; the genius thinks.

In order to raise children to be mature or existentially free, we would have to take them away from their parents and educate them individually not collectively. The current system is self-perpetuating: If parents and education remain, the insecurity will linger.

We think that because we are educated, we are mature. Not necessarily. The conformist education can only take you so far.

The first goal of life should be to find yourself. Success should be being happy for who you are.

Education makes caterpillars out of us; it takes a highly curious individual to become a butterfly.

"Educating the mind without educating the heart is no education at all." - Aristotle.

We get exposed to the herd through parenthood and education and we learn: Make other people happy in order to make yourself happy. The extreme end of this is the insecure individual who gets it into their head they need to be famous in order to be happy. Fame to them means mass approval by millions if not billions. They become famous and a couple of years later commit suicide because of the pressure of being known.

What education does is it makes us oblivious to perceiving people as threats. We become so used to knowing people that it becomes second nature to us to meet people. Instead of seeing people as threats to one's security, we see them as a necessity. In other words, one instinctively says that they need to know people in order to be happy. The reality is (and I allude to it throughout these notes) that you need to be less known to be more secure. You need to be anonymous to be truly free. I admit that it sounds so absurd and alien to the current model of existence but that is only because of the extent of the brainwashing you are subjected to when young.

Capitalism is a conglomerate of insecurity. You make people insecure. You have parents who tell you how to behave; you then are educated and again told how to behave; you then must work and again are told how to behave. You make people interact with each other, which in turn makes them fear each other, which in turn makes them insecure, which in turn makes them conform, which in turn is the crankshaft of the economic world as we know it to be.

"The whole educational and professional training system is a very elaborate filter, which just weeds out people who are too independent, and who think for themselves, and who don't know how to be submissive, and so on -- because they're dysfunctional to the institutions." - Noam Chomsky.

Look at what our average adolescents are doing. They are not in the library at the weekend reading about how to change the world. More than likely they are walking through the shopping centre looking for clothes or gadgets to buy. Why are they doing this? They are because society has through various mechanisms told them to be obsessed with being desired. This is the Capitalistic Insecurity.

Parenthood is like the educational system, the prisons, the mental institutions and so on. It is part of the regulation of the individual.

Being ambitious is not wrong; but being ambitious for the sake of improving your image is the wrong reason to be ambitious.

In order to understand the world, you must distance yourself from it on occasion.

Such is the system that human beings are bred to enjoy making millions for someone else.

We are born geniuses and educated to be mediocre.

Intelligent life from another galaxy would look at our colleges and schools and say they are factories of obedience. This is where we program the machines to behave a certain way.

The current system teaches us to learn what has already been learned. It doesn't teach us to learn what has yet to be learned.

You bombard the innocent mind of the child with propaganda pertaining towards love and work and thus they grow up with this system deep rooted in their unconscious mind. It becomes familiar to them as Mere Exposure Theory suggests. Another part of the brainwashing is to convince them that they are free and as such "living," by adopting this model. So marrying and work becomes part and parcel of life. It really is astonishing at how easy the system decides the system and part of the problem is the average person is in denial that they have been manipulated.

I said in previous notes that one of the most frightening aspects of the human being is just how easily we can be manipulated, and this flaw has a huge bearing on conformity.

Such is the pattern in life you would swear we are living in a matrix, wherein all our wants and wills are coded into us. We thus become obsessed with love and work because that is how we are written by the higher power. They make everyone's face different but their mind the same.

"We are all in a post-hypnotic trance induced in early infancy." - RD Laing.

It is easier to fool society than convince them they have been fooled.

I remember a serial killer once remarked that the reason he was able to kill so many through gaining their trust was in the fact that people don't see other people as threats. We instinctively see other people as safe or reliable.

People are threats not in a violent sense, but in an existential sense. The whole pattern we observe in society is a response not to freedom, but to fear. We think that through parenthood and education we can make a child compassionate, but we also inadvertently make them insecure. When you expose man to the herd be it school or social media, he becomes afraid. Conformity, narcissism, morality etc. they are all a response to fear.

When the insecure individual thinks of solitude they think of a negative interpretation from the herd.

Think about it. No one ever comes out and tells their parents they are going to live alone. There is an onus on the individual that they will get married or at least try to. This is how the system sustains itself. You condition children to want to live a certain way and when they grow up they do their all to realize this.

Gratitude is the most sublime education of all.

I would much rather live in a world with education than one without it. Education does produce a compassionate and humane society. But a negative by product of it, is insecurity.

Conformity

"The desire to be yourself is the true vocation of being human." - Rollo May.

The unconscious response to being labelled is conformity. Conformity is a direct product of being known and being labelled. Interpretation (the fear of being labelled) moulds society as much as money or desire or religion.

Again, Normative Social Influence says part of the reason we conform is to be liked. In other words, we conform to be labelled positively.

Sartre called it Bad Faith. We are so afraid of being negatively labelled by society should we choose to deviate from conformity, that we are condemned to conform. This is particularly the case of the narcissist. They are so afraid of negative labels that they play the role of a husband/wife or father/mother. They are not authentic to themselves. They wilt to societal pressures purely so they can be idolized.

When you walk down a street, your interpretation controls society, but society is in turn controlling you. But you do not perceive it as such because it is unconscious.

We are all mad; but madness practiced by a majority is considered normality. Conformity is a madness.

An organized delusion is a normalized delusion. Psychiatric illness is relative.

Men and women repress millions of years of evolution just to appease the herd. Your freedom if anything is your enthusiasm to defy the people you love.

The want to be attractive or desirable would be classified as a mental illness if it were not both a necessity for economies and practised by the majority.

A battle has been raging since the dawn of mankind. Between what the male of society wants and what the female of society wants, and the outcome is conformity.

Madness is following sports teams. Madness is following religion. Madness is believing in true love. But all these things are practised by billions and because of this they become satisfactory.

We are all convicted conformists.

Insanity is renovating your kitchen purely for aesthetic reasons; insanity is making the rich richer; insanity is trying to be desirable. But because these things feed an economy, they are considered normal.

What we have in life is a case of the rich telling the blind how to make them rich.

We use freedom to radicalize the hearts of men.

We leverage our happiness on another person and in doing so reject our individual self as sufficient. That is why there is so much unhappiness.

Conformity begets conformity; the herd radicalizes the next generation.

We know everything about Einstein but nothing about his universe. We know everything about Manchester United or Kim Kardashian but are completely blind to the true nature of this universe. I call this Economic Narcissism. We are normalized on the world we see with our eyes, so much, that the true world is ignored. Work, love, sport, music, sex, money, whatever you say, it is all an illusion, but it is our illusion.

What I mean by "Economic Narcissism," is someone who is not necessarily a full-blown narcissist, but who has been raised in such a way, that they only see work and relationships and hence are blind to the universe. Most people are corrupted by this Economic Narcissism. Life to them is two dimensional, in that it is work and relationships. They do not see the universe or the quantum mechanics of the atom. They only see work and relationships (and other things) and thus are immature and often insecure because of it.

Economic Narcissism is vital for the system to thrive. People see work as normal. They see relationships as necessary. They do not see other people as threats. They are encouraged to associate with the herd. Any behaviour considered deviant is criminalized. We have what is good and we have what is bad. All the while they cannot see the universe. The system depends on the illusion of life sustaining itself through this Economic Narcissism. It is implemented when young. We do not teach children about the futility of it all. We brainwash them to believe they have not been brainwashed.

The Economic Narcissism leads to either Mature or Immature Conformity and which then blinds the individual to the universe.

Why are people so willing to invest so much time, money and most importantly, happiness, on a football team? The football player, I can understand why he does it, for he makes millions. But what does the average football fan get? He feels good for a couple of hours when his team wins. Karl Marx would be turning in his grave. Then apply the same reason to relationships, movie stars, work, family, friends, holidays etc. The existential question, then is, why cannot you just be grateful to be alive in this universe. Why not make the fact that you are alive, your happiness? Think of the infinite number of people who have never had the ability to taste existence in this universe.

No one looks at a popular sport like football and sees the idiosyncrasies of it. Their mind has become acclimatized to its rules and behaviour. Intelligent life from another galaxy would find it strange, initially, until they too become normalized on it. Similarly, with the economic system of relationships and work. Nobody sees these things as oppression or authoritarian; they see them as normal and things that you just do.

There are two worlds: One of anarchy and one of insanity. Anarchy is if the world was ending in a week's time; insanity is the world as we know it.

Society suffers to be moral; the disease is fear; the symptom is conformity. This is due to the threat of labelling.

Why doesn't psychiatry declare religion a madness?

I would wager we are the most intelligent species in this universe or any universe and yet we all function the same way.

Remember what Arthur Schopenhauer said: "We take the limits of our field of vision to be the limits of the world." In that spirit, being in a relationship and working are things we have come to accept as normal. The schizophrenic is labelled insane; the individual who conforms implicitly is regarded as a valued member of society. We cannot fathom the insanity of being in love or working because we are conditioned to it.

What we define as madness is relative. There are no rules in this nihilistic universe. What we call schizophrenia could be euphoria in another world. A relationship involving two people is neither right nor wrong, but it is convenient.

Why don't they teach psychology in schools I have always wondered?

What you will do with your life boils down to three choices: You can be a criminal, a conformist or an individual. Every lifestyle falls under one of those three brackets.

Ask yourself what motivates the legions of men and women to bend to gender norms?

If intelligent life from another galaxy were to observe mankind, they would deduce a few things. They would see an animal that has learned to reason but attests to himself that he cannot be happy unless he is loved by another person. This is macro-scale insanity. That we exclaim to ourselves we cannot be happy until we are loved is a form of madness.

Normality is statistically relative. It depends on the perception of the herd and how many of the herd think that way.

If only one in a hundred fell in love, then love would be the psychosis.

To believe in god is to be religious; to hear voices from that same god is to be schizophrenic. If I feel the presence of god, I am a saint; if I listen to what god says to me, I am sent to the asylum. One loses faith with psychiatry when they fail to diagnose the belief in the divine as a psychiatric illness. And what of love? Should the individual who refuses to be happy until they are in love not be classified as psychiatrically ill? The law-abiding member of society is classed as an esteemed man or woman. In a parallel world he or she is deemed a psychological heretic. What we determine to be healthy behaviour is not a fundamental constant of nature. It depends on what the herd decides is acceptable.

The free world as we understand it is the asylum. The lie is that you must "live" in order to live.

"Most people die at 25 and are not buried until they are 75." - Benjamin Franklin.

There is a contradiction with regards money. We need it to pay for our health insurance, but in earning money we neglect our health. Then when we are awash with lots of money, but our health is declining we pour all our earned money into our health to try and prolong it. But it is too late to tend to ourselves.

Imagine a foreign world in another galaxy, where there is a cultural phenomenon that makes its inhabitants obsess with being in the company of another person and being approved by the person to be happy. Thus, their whole life is built around finding this other person and one cannot be happy until they have found this said person. Us humans, analysing this world would think it is a terrible system. Yet this is precisely what happens on earth. Insecure men and especially women remark to themselves that they cannot be happy in this universe until they are in love and have found this special person. It is a narcissistic disease that infects the individual when young and consequently is arguably the prime source of unhappiness within the individual.

"Great things are not accomplished by those who yield to trends and fads and popular opinion." - Jack Kerouac.

Take an impromptu hike through a busy city street and you will discern madness all around you.

Within exposure comes regulation. Regulation is the by-product of exposure. So what is exposure? It is going to school or to work in an office. It is being on social media. It is meeting up with friends on the weekend. All these things lead inevitably to adherence to society's principles.

We take what we see for granted. No one ever questions why an attractive woman is lauded for her appearance. Why not castigate her for being attractive? Why don't we live in a world where love was a crime and working were capital-punishment? The power of conformity (the will to conform) casts an enormous shadow over society. Men are told to be men and women are told to be women and they suffer instinctively.

The economic system does not directly tell people how to behave. That would be authoritarian. What it does is suggest, rather sneakily, how to become happy. Low and behold, this being happy benefits the economic system.

What did psychiatrists like RD Laing, Rollo May and Erich Fromm say? They said just because billions of people do or want the same things, does not make those billions of people sane. What we come to regard as life, is in ways an illusion, but one that benefits the economic system. In the vastness of the universe, where else will you find love and work?

The shrewdest component is not the lie but rather who tells it. The government does not have to brainwash society because it gets parents, doctors, teachers, celebrities, films, books, music and so on, to brainwash the next generation.

The propaganda pertaining towards relationships is relentless. Parents, friends, doctors, psychologists, magazines, books, films all show or emphasize people in love. The individual is drowned in so much propaganda that they believe it unconditionally. It becomes familiar to them instinctively through the Mere Exposure Theory. In other words, they become brainwashed. In order to be labelled correctly by the herd, they must conform.

This material or commoditized happiness destroys man. This symbol of happiness through relationships, families, work, friendship, commodities etc. ultimately prevents man from being happy.

"Almost all of our sorrowing's spring out of our relations with other people." - Arthur Schopenhauer.

Being an individual is what torments man.

We effectively rape society through our eyes and our opinions. That is why men must be men and women must be women.

The system by telling you how to live also tells you how to be happy.

You never hear the powers that be state that if only you avoided interaction you could live a simple life. Interaction is a necessity for the human condition and economies, but the by-product of it is that people fall out.

Society is putting society under pressure. You don't see the effects, but you experience them. To use the analogy, no one sees space time, but its effect on a planet is observed (the planet locks into orbit). Nobody tells you: Do this or do that. But silently they instruct you to. You respond instinctively to pacify them. You respond instinctively to be labelled correctly.

We have more money but less wealth; more food but less comfort; more friends but less friendship.

"How in the hell could a man enjoy being awakened at 8.30 am by an alarm clock, leap out of bed, dress, force-feed, shit, piss, brush teeth and hair, and fight traffic to get to a place where essentially you made lots of money for somebody else and were asked to be grateful for the opportunity to do so?" - Charles Bukowski.

Self-Perception Theory says that behaviours determine attitudes. In other words, what we do, determines how we think. It is counter intuitive. Imagine a man who has sexual liaisons with other men. He says to himself, "I am having sex with men, therefore I must be homosexual." Whereas traditional thought says that a man thinks he is homosexual (his attitude) and then has sex with men (his behaviour) because of that attitude. Likewise, it can be applied to conformity and Pretence Happiness. "I have the job, the family, the nice house, the fast car, the two holidays a year, therefore I must be happy. I look happy through behaving like this; therefore I must be happy." Accumulating X, Y and Z is his behaviour. This then leads to an attitude, that he must be happy because of it. Often because of this, we feign happiness. We pretend to be happy. This is Pretence Happiness brought on by Self-Perception Theory.

Isn't the coincidence beautiful. What benefits the individual also benefits the economic system. I am being facetious because it is not coincidence; it is the way the system is set up. It is Self-Perception Theory or at least a variation of it. The individual is told: "This is how you behave." You meet friends, you work, you have sex, you marry, you have children etc. Then because this is their behaviour, they formulate an attitude whereby this set of behaviours must be correct. They then feign happiness.

The individual is told that you become happy through work and relationships, both which greatly benefit the economic system. Then they convince themselves that they are happy in doing these things because they are doing them. It is Self-Perception Theory.

Cognitive Dissonance can also be applied to the young man or woman. They go out and get a job and get a relationship. They find themselves under stress and that the dream life has not materialized as planned. There exists a sort of conflict. They are living "the good life" except they are not happy. To reduce their cognitive dissonance, they then exclaim, "once I am forty and have the family and have advanced in my career, then I will be happy."

Cognitive Dissonance: The young twenty-year old is working long hours and for a low wage. "Once I am thirty and have this and that, then I will be happy." Then they reach thirty and have to pay bills and so on. "Once I am forty, then I will be happy." Then they reach forty and have children to look after. Can you see where I am going with this. In order to reduce their cognitive dissonance, they are all the time looking towards this dream life in the future. "Once I have X, Y and Z, then I will be happy." Do they become permanently happy? No, because their happiness is fleeting, in that it never lasts. This leads to another thing social psychologists call Affective Forecasting and it especially applies to the dream life. Affective Forecasting is the theory that says, happiness does not last. Just as you think that once you have the dream existence, you will be permanently happy. You will not. You will just want more.

Think about it. Ask yourself: "How much of my time and money is spent in trying to make people like me?" You get a haircut, you buy new clothes, you wear perfume, you drive a fancy car, you get an esteemed job etc. All these things are behaviours designed (in part) to make you more desirable to your partner, your parents and the herd. Then contemplate this: "What if I stopped caring about being liked?" What if you did not care what your parents, friends and co-workers thought of you? Wouldn't you have more time, more money and most importantly more happiness. This is the cusp of the Capitalistic Insecurity. Such an individual does not worry about food, shelter or warmth. They have all those things in abundance and yet they still are beset with anxiety. What is the nature of this anxiety? Simply, they fear not being liked.

We are told when young how to behave and what to want. Then as we mature into adults, we try to engineer what we are told. Parents and education effectively tell us that this is the system we choose. Then because we are insecure, we do our utmost to adopt the system to make parents and our peers happy. Why are men and women obsessed with love? Why not be obsessed with solitude? They are because they are taught to be in youth and not because it is an instinctive drive of the human condition. You impregnate the young individuals mind with love propaganda. Everywhere he or she looks they see people in relationships and thus sees no other option.

Think of the Islamist fundamentalist who blows himself up in the name of his religion. He does so because he has been so brainwashed. Now apply that same mechanism to the individual who must find love, get married and have children. They have been completely brainwashed from a very young age.

"The mass of men lead lives of quiet desperation." - Henry David Thoreau.

There is something grossly wrong with the system if the homeless man who sits by the bridge is happier than the average working man or woman.

Think about it: When was the last time in the midst of work and relationships that you thought about the scope of the universe? Or have you ever even contemplated this existential question? Right now, as you read these notes, you are through the effects of space time contained on a planet, which in turn is revolving around a star, which is in turn revolving around a black hole at the centre of the galaxy and the galaxy in turn is flying through space. We never think such alienated thoughts and truth be told the powers that be don't want us to think like this, because when you do, you realize how futile everything in the world as you know it is.

You are entitled to your own opinion, no doubt, but you are not entitled to your own facts.

The system is astute, very astute. It tells you what to do and then convinces you that you are making your own decisions. Society is really like another person that lectures us on how to behave.

Relationships and careers work off each other. People need to work to be in a relationship. If they are not working, they are less attractive to potential partners. Then when they enter into a relationship, they need to work to fund that relationship.

The question one should ask is not why we believe, but rather why we are so easily manipulated to believe. There must be something nuclear at work if you can take the most intelligent life force in this universe and make them all want the same things. And it all starts when you are young and in education.

The herd asks: "When are you getting married? When are you having children?" Questions like these only serve to put the individual under pressure to conform. The insecure of society must understand that they are not getting married or rearing children because they just want to do these things. They are in part under so much pressure to get married and to rear children. They live in fear of a negative opinion.

"We have multiplied our possessions but reduced our values. We talk too much, love too seldom, and hate too often. We've learned how to make a living, but not a life; we've added years to life, not life to years." - Dr Bob Moorehead (The Paradox of our Time.)

Fear is a huge reason why we conform. Imagine the individual that tells their parents they do not want to get married; the parents will remark that that individual is letting down the family. That same individual tells friends that they do not want to get married; the friends will probably distance themselves from him or her. That same individual tells co-workers they do not want to get married; the co-workers then laugh at him or her. We are afraid and we have been afraid since a young age.

That we can speak means we can think and consequently we apply an egocentric view to ourselves as a species. Then in our desperation to possess meaning as humans we have engineered religion and true love among other things.

Man is the only animal who has the luxury of being aware of the universe and yet he still must wilt to his animalistic instincts. It is just these instincts are relationships and careers.

Solitude is the only true freedom in this world. The anonymity that accompanies solitude can liberate you. It is only in being unknown can you truly be who you want to be.

The floodwaters of conformity drown our youth; you can either choose to flow with them or stand against them.

The brainwashed narcissistic conformist when told about the callous nihilistic universe becomes hostile. Life to them is relationships and careers. They cannot be lectured on the insubstantial nature of relationships and careers. Open your eyes. The world is not the blue skies and the friendships; it is not the ability to love or work in an exemplary job; the world is the universe of which we are incredibly lucky to exist in.

We use the institution of the family to indoctrinate men and women to procreate.

Only with the apocalypse imminent would society become free.

For the system to work, you need a million conformists for every rebel.

The herd has such a sway over society. It has the power to make the insecure individual happy or sad. When the herd approves of the individual, he or she feels content. But when they disapprove of the individual, he or she feels dejected. This is Normative Social Influence.

You must ask yourself honestly: Are you getting married because this is what you wish to do or is it because you are trying to appease the tribe?

It is not a question of how long you live but rather how much living you do with the life you have.

Conformity has become in a Darwinian sense the means by which the species survives. If you told society in an almost Soviet method to procreate, have children and provide for the economy, they would reject that system outright. If you force them to marry and raise a family, they more than likely will not. But call that system love or romance and they casually accept it without hesitation. Of course, it helps when you brainwash them in education to adopt the system. But the two propositions are entirely the same, we just perceive them differently. In one system, it is called oppression; in the other system, it is called living.

The economic system is one of oppression. The free world of work and relationships is the penitentiary. But this oppression is neutralized by the seductive nature of true love and money. We see these things as part of being free.

The extent of the manipulation is hard for the individual to recognise. But if you look at a religious fundamentalist or the devotion of North Korea to its leader and then apply that to a simple law-abiding citizen who wishes to work and love, you come to realize its power. It is just this conformist manipulation is portrayed as righteous and a necessity. The heart-breaking truth is it is not. There are no rules. There is no god or true love or anything. There is only absolute absurdness.

Whichever system prevails is a function of the herd and not because it is universally correct.

When you champion yourself, you are no longer imprisoned by the need to be championed by another.

Rollo May: "We suffer from the fear of finding ourselves alone, that we never find ourselves at all."

There is always a next generation of criminals and likewise conformists. We are all puppets dancing to the strings of conformity.

You will only be remembered if you are a genius, good looking or a criminal, or perhaps all three.

In this world of facebook and social media, people impulsively compute that the more people in their life, the better, but the opposite is actually true, in that the less people in your life, the less volatile it becomes. We need less friends and more friendship.

"If Epicurus were speaking to you at this moment, he would urge you to simplify life. Here's how he might put it if he were standing here today: " Lads, your needs are few, they are easily attained, and any necessary suffering can be easily tolerated. Don't complicate your life with such trivial goals as riches and fame: they are the enemy of ATARAXIA. Fame, for example, consists of the opinions of others and requires that we must live our life as others wish. To achieve and maintain fame, we must like what others like and shun whatever it is that they shun. Hence, a life of fame or a life in politics? Flee from it. And wealth? Avoid it! It is a trap. The more we acquire the more we crave, and the deeper our sadness when our yearning is not satisfied. Lads, listen to me: If you crave happiness, do not waste your life struggling for that which you really do not need." - Irvin Yalom.

I look at the modern-day man and woman and I sense fear. They are afraid to be individuals.

So commoditized is the life of the individual. It is freedom in their teens, exploring in their twenties, marriage in their thirties, children in their forties, promotions in their fifties, retirement in their sixties, grandchildren in their seventies, death in their eighties. Look at a million people and the majority will convey this pattern. This is the most intelligent species the universe has ever given birth to and they all live such fashionable lives.

Obscurity rhymes with conformity.

We think that because we are born to parents, that this automatically defines us as free. But this is all part of the indoctrination when young. Imagine for instance you were born in the laboratory; you would not ascertain that you are free. The same should apply to the system of birth in the present day.

In adolescence, we become a servant of gratification. We need the material life in order to feel good about ourselves. As such we become addicted to being gratified, be it emotional, financial, sexual or image based. But to be gratified means in a Schopenhauer method that you must suffer and to suffer in my philosophy is to not enjoy life. A more concrete happiness is gratitude. You do not suffer to be grateful.

We need less money and more wealth, less friends and more friendship, less love and more compassion.

"Modern man has transformed himself into a commodity; he experiences his life energy as an investment with which he should make the highest profit, considering his position and the situation on the personality market. He is alienated from himself, from his fellow men and from nature. His main aim is profitable exchange of his skills, knowledge, and of himself, his "personality package" with others who are equally intent on a fair and profitable exchange. Life has no goal except the one to move, no principle except the one of fair exchange, no satisfaction except the one to consume." - Erich Fromm.

Man is alienated from the universe.

The power of this persuasion is intense. For example, to use an analogy: Advertising. Adverts work by bombarding our unconscious mind with the same jargon. They play the same ad on television for an extended period. Eventually this ad becomes lodged in your unconscious. Then in the supermarket you buy this new product that you have never bought before, and you think that you consciously made a decision to purchase it. This is false. What has happened is your unconscious mind has manipulated you into buying the product. Now one must apply this to conformity, but the real world is the television in this case. Your mind is bombarded with propaganda pertaining towards conformity. You see people in relationships, you see people adapting their behaviour to meet gender constraints; you see people working and paying mortgages. Your mind becomes manipulated or radicalized into wanting to live a certain way. To be existentially mature or existentially free is to challenge this persuasion. In other words, you rewire your brain to want differently.

One must distinguish between Mature Conformity and Immature Conformity. Immature Conformity is desperation. Such a person has been taught from a noticeably young age that they must be doing A, B and C in order to be of value. Such individuals are narcissistic and insecure. In contrast, Mature Conformity is where the individual recognises that they have many choices available to them in life. They are not corrupted by the herd. They are not narcissistic.

Immature Conformity is when the male/female is afraid of not being a husband/wife and father/mother.

Mature Conformity is confidence; Immature Conformity is fear.

Immature conformity leads to the belief in true love.

I especially observe this amongst the poorer or working-class society. They are so afraid of being different and being the odd one out that they are forced to conform. This is Immature Conformity.

Guilt leads to Immature Conformity. You make the individual feel guilty about missing out on life. You make them feel guilty about not having sex, not being in love, not having a family, not working this dream job and so on. This makes them conform. But it is Immature Conformity because they are so afraid of missing out in life.

The mature conformists remark that they can do A or B or C; the immature conformists remark that they have to do A.

The healthy position is that you say you can be married or have a partner, but that it is not vital that you do so. This is Mature Conformity. The unhealthy position is desperation, in that you have to have a partner, as if your life depends on it. This is Immature Conformity. Such a person thinks this way because society has taught them to think this way. They then look at other people, who seem to have it all and yearn for the same themselves. They then are afraid of what people will think of them if they do not conform.

Immature Conformity: What do immature and insecure people ask? They ask, "how do men behave?" Or, "how do women behave?" They then just play the role of that said man or woman as Erving Goffman would attest.

Immature Conformity uses narcissism to fuel one's existence. Mature Conformity replaces this narcissism with gratitude. One's existence may stay the same, but their attitude changes. The trick is being grateful as you are gratified.

The difference is fear. Mature conformists are not frightened; immature conformists are.

What you do in life, you do because you can, not because you must do it.

The commoditized relationship in one sentence: They need to be in a relationship because they need to be seen in one. You see it amongst adolescents because they are immature. You also see it amongst famous people because they are known by the whole world and as such under pressure.

The ability to live alone is the first sign of maturity.

"Every human being must have a point at which he stands against the culture, where he says, this is me and the damned world can go to hell." - Rollo May

To be led is to be misled. Every four years I observe the presidential elections in the United States. The chosen candidate stands in front of an arena full of spectators and they are all cheering him or her on. Do you think that the potential president cares one iota for these people? Fat chance. That is not cynicism; that is the cold reality. We see it with sports stars, film stars, religious leaders etc. They become idolized, they manipulate their chosen audience and that is how they build their empire. The individual just has no idea, not even a modicum of curiosity, as to how easy they are to manipulate. And to be mature is to realize that. You may still vote for them, but you have the wisdom to realize that they don't care a dime about you.

What does social media do? It unconsciously manipulates the individual into mimicking the collective. It is doing the exact same thing education did to us when we were young. The guys must be successful and confident; the girls must be attractive; both must have sex, marry and have children; this is how you are approved. It is easy to blame the government and such an opinion is naïve. The true reality is that society is determining society through virtue of the fact that you expose the individuals in society to each other.

They manipulate you to conform by not telling you to conform. By not telling you overtly, you come to believe that it is your own choice.

You fear your parents as much as the predator. They covertly if not overtly tell you how to live.

You must remove yourself from the perception that a relationship is the right way, the correct way and the only way. You have been brainwashed to hold such a disposition through education, parents, friends etc.

We are so normalized and acclimatized to life that we just can't see the laboratory that is human existence. It would take intelligent life from another galaxy to point it out to us, such is our ego and denial. We use men and women as breeding machines to keep the system afloat; we educate children to induce them to conform; we make them work in jobs they don't like so that economics will prevail; we pollute their minds with propaganda that encourages them to marry. The fact that we are humans, can speak and are smart is irrelevant. We are being used like machines on a farm. The earth as we know it is a giant concentration camp and the free citizens are its prisoners.

We determine our own choices said Sartre, yet so many are prescribed choice by the environment, and it's called conformity.

We call it artificial insemination on the farm; in the human fabricated world, it's called life.

Just like the rules of war are constructed to ensure soldiers do not turn back from the enemy fire, the rules of economies are constructed to subjugate men and women. They take out a financial and psychological mortgage with regards a house and family respectively and then must slave their whole lives to make those loans mature. You enslave them with debt, be it financial or emotional. This is exactly what the powers that be wish of people; that they work, take out a mortgage and have a family because this is what keeps the system alive, just as soldiers must die to win the war. The irony is that the people think they are free. They are filled with so much propaganda with regards this luxury of "living," of working this esteemed job, of becoming a parent, that they cannot see the slavery.

Those in concentration camps have a will to survive, despite the deplorable conditions. Yet so many commit suicide in the free markets of North America, Asia, Europe and so on. To an outside observer, they would conclude that the economic system we are so inured on is a system of tyranny. But the average individual cannot see this.

Of course, some see through the deception. They become financially independent when young; they choose not to get married to placate the peer pressure.

One must see the similarities between freedom and social control. Society instinctively thinks that they are free and that is why they choose what they choose. This is false. They are told through social control this is what you choose and because their unconscious mind becomes so absorbed in it, they think they are making their own choices and hence they think they are free.

Such is the persuasion we like a person who we know other people will like. Our whole lives become about image.

In the totalitarian country we fear the government; in the free world we fear each other.

A man worked at a factory. Every night he would wheel his empty wheelbarrow out of the factory past the guards. The boss of the factory suspected him of stealing something and so had the guards check the wheelbarrow and pat the man down. Every night this happened and every night the guards could not find anything. However, the man was stealing something: Wheelbarrows. The point I am trying to make is that sometimes your mind is so inured on something and it cannot see the obvious and this is essentially why conformity thrives. Your unconscious mind is so hardwired on work and relationships that they become normal things to do. Conforming is the existential wheelbarrow.

Think about it. Why do most men and women statistically get married in their thirties? Why not their teens or seventies? They do so because society has effectively told them to do so. They are like machines such is the pattern. They are no better than the lambs bred for the spring slaughter.

The conformist lives for the future but the outstanding irony is that the future only brings us closer to death.

As the Dalai Lama said, we aim for retirement and as such misuse the better part of our lives. There is nothing beyond this life despite what we are led to believe. "One shot," says Robert De Niro's character in The Deer Hunter and that is all this life is. When you think like that you become grateful and thus become happy.

There is a conflict raging in the hearts of men, between what we want the universe to represent and what it actually represents.

Jack Kerouac's On The Road should be read by everyone, especially when they are in adolescence.

It is interesting to ascertain who has been manipulated; what is even more interesting is why they have been manipulated; but what is most interesting is how they were manipulated.

It's a concentration camp without barbed wire. In the camp we fear the guards; in the free world we fear each other. The whole system thrives on latently telling people that by doing this or behaving a certain way you are in fact "living." So, by marrying, you are "living." By having children, you are "living." By working till you are sixty-five, you are "living." Through looking attractive, you are "living." Through buying things you do not need, you are "living." Just like in the concentration camp you are told to do this and that, in the free world you are told how to conduct yourself. The difference is that in the free world this is seen as part of the fabric of "living." And people then become so brainwashed on this model that they heed to it instinctively. They never even question what they are doing, let alone understand why they do it.

The average individual is under severe pressure to be an average individual.

"I do not know what I may appear to the world, but to myself I seem to have been only like a boy playing on the seashore, and diverting myself in now and then finding a smoother pebble or a prettier shell than ordinary, whilst the great ocean of truth lay all undiscovered before me."- Issac Newton.

Faith is the natural antidote to the venom of truth.

I hear a common complaint about this idealistic life is that the individual needs to work to provide for their family. But family is a psychological mortgage just like buying a house is a financial one. It's just society is so inured on having a family and see it as a necessary component of existence. They can't even bear entertain the thought that they shouldn't have a family. The reality is that if you didn't have a family you would have so much more autonomy to do what you actually want to do in this world.

Traditional thinking says we do things because we want to. Nihilistic thinking says we do things because we are afraid.

Our parents are the most abusive people in our lives.

The animal responds to fear. A gazelle tries to escape a cheetah. Humans respond to fear also. But they also respond to embarrassment. They try not to be laughed at; they try to be positively labelled.

Many are aware that they are being manipulated by the adverts on tv; few are aware that they are being manipulated by real life itself. I repeat it, that we see so many getting married and having children, it becomes through Normative Social Influence, the correct method to live or behave. Capitalism essentially markets itself through itself. The rich coerce the poor; the confident coerce the anxious; the successful people coerce the failures; the beautiful people coerce the ugly; the celebrities coerce the nobodies. We look at the esteemed patrons of capitalism and we think: "If only I had what they had, then I would be happy."

The two threats, one is sociological or economic and the other is existential. The first one, we fear being negatively labelled. If we do not have sex or get married people will laugh at us. The second one we fear not living life to the fullest. If we do not have sex or get married, we will somehow waste our lives. If you are living to neutralize one or both threats, you are living for the wrong reasons.

Facebook, Instagram, social media, are all instruments of labelling. They all induce the Labelling Anxiety within people because they all have to post pictures and what not, of a specific life, in order to be labelled positively. Now apply that same reason to one's life outside of social media. We finely tune our existence to be labelled positively from friends, parents, neighbours and co-workers. Now this is not all bad. Labelling produces a law-abiding society; but the negatives of it are insecurity and narcissism.

It is hard to reconcile the necessity of the system with its failure. How many have committed suicide because of the system? How many take out a financial and psychological mortgage and then implode under its pressure? The system despite being a prerequisite for the world we know it as, is not perfect and society should be made aware of this schism.

We essentially become habitual gratification whores. We go into work anxious and we either walk out still anxious or glad because we succeeded in some way. The next day we do the exact thing, as we do the next week or year or decade. Daily life becomes a battle between anxiety and gratification. As such we waste so much of our existence in feeling unwell.

I am not the first to say this; Schopenhauer said it, as did Nietzsche, as did Marcus Aurelius and Sartre; as do psychiatrists and economists. If you want to be happy, do not get married and have children; learn to live alone and you can avoid so much stress. It also begs the question that why don't the powers that be come out and say this? Why don't the politicians, CEOs, the religious leaders and so on, promote living alone to minimize stress and to be happy? They don't because the family is the nucleus of the economic system. They need people to get married and have children to sustain the system.

We all dream of changing the world, but usually the world changes us.

Our minds become so intrigued or outraged at anything that deviates from the archetype of conformity that we ignore the pattern of conformity.

Our hunter gatherer relatives worried about food, warmth and predators. Society today worries about money and image. Future civilization I would hope would be living in a system without worry, whatever system that may be. Perhaps and I hope this isn't true, the only viable system in which society doesn't worry is one in which there is no society.

Most people are not even afraid of losing their life. What they are afraid of is losing their home, their partner, their family or their job. That alone is a severe damnation of the current economic system.

Dale Carnegies book is probably both the most popular and most highly selling self-help book in existence and the central theme of it is about winning people or making them like you. Alas in my opinion this is your fatal mistake and an enormous reason why people are unhappy and veer between gladness and unhappiness on a daily cycle. If you approach each day through trying to be endorsed or approbated by the people in your life, well then it is obvious that you will be anxious. Why? You will be anxious because you are dependent on people's interpretation of you to be content. When they are pleased by you, like you or endorse you, you thus feel glowing. But what of when they reject you? How do you feel then? This is the carcinogenic nature of the current system wherein we are forced to make people happy (be they partners, friends, co-workers or parents,) in order to make ourselves happy.

The irony of these notes is that I still have not introduced a system where everything is perfect. I can rid the anxiety of relationships by suggesting that the individual lives in solitude. But what with regards the anxiety of working? People do need to earn money to possess a good standard of living. Perhaps in the future the schism or split between work and stress can be negated.

"Truth always rests with the minority, and the minority is always stronger than the majority, because the minority is generally formed by those who really have an opinion, while the strength of a majority is illusory, formed by the gangs who have no opinion" - Soren Kierkegaard.

We do not teach our children to be grateful because gratitude does not benefit the system as much as narcissism.

When the brainwashing benefits the system, we do not call it brainwashing.

The scientist's question what we take for granted. So too must the young conformist.

Our unconscious minds are absolutely terrified of non-conforming to the point that we are absolutely unconsciously terrified of being an individual.

What is a friend? One who can tolerate you and you them.

Individuality is the price we pay for acceptance.

We are not afraid of being laughed at by a kangaroo. Nor a hippopotamus, nor an ant, nor a bacterium. In fact, there is only one animal we are afraid of being laughed at and that is our fellow human beings. When you understand that you can understand a lot of human behaviour because this said behaviour is just a response to this threat of laughter. Yes, we are governed by desire; yes, we are governed by finance; but we are also governed by laughter.

We are slaves, slaves to each other.

Do not doubt the veracity of Jean Paul Sartre's statement: "Hell is other people." Throughout my research, within those suffering from depression and anxiety, a common denominator is "other people." The boss is causing them stress; their partner is making covert threats and so on. The very "people" we are told to depend on are the very ones that make existence unbearable.

I remember a college lecturer once remarked that he said something so outlandish and ridiculous and passed if off as scientific fact to his students and the students proceeded to write down the notes. He then at the end of the year reported to the students that the bizarre lecture he gave was actually false and that he had made it up to demonstrate how gullible and easily manipulated people are. The point he was trying to make is that people invariably believe what they are told and this applies to conformity. Very seldom do people have the inquisitiveness and courage to question why they conform. They just heed to what society tells them and pass it off as fact.

As Durkheim may remark, the freedom that capitalism affords, is not necessarily a good thing because we can be our own worst enemies, such is the pressure we put on ourselves. The bigger the dream, the worst the nightmare when things go wrong.

We are told how brilliant western civilization and capitalism is. Yet more people commit suicide in these countries. So, something is seriously wrong with the system. Durkheim wrote a book about this a 100-years ago and not a lot has changed.

"Normality is a paved road. It is comfortable to walk on, but no flowers grow on it." - Vincent Van Gogh.

In failure, your life can fall apart or fall together.

Imagine a concentration camp the size of America. In this camp people are told to "work" to help maintain the camp of which they get paid a bursary to which they can spend on food or buying stuff for their cell they call their "home." However, they must receive a loan from the authorities to pay for their cell which is called a "mortgage." This way they are enslaved with debt and must work in the system. They are also told to find a partner as soon as they reach a certain age and to procreate. They are brainwashed to call this relationship "love." Men are told to look confident and strong; the women are told to appear sexual and enticing. They then are forced to have "children" to sustain the camp. Women are effectively used as breeding machines to keep the system afloat and this is called "becoming a mother." Furthermore, once they have children the parents are told to put pressure on the children to become parents themselves and to work in the camp. Also, a system of brainwashing called "education" is enacted to mould children a certain way so that when they mature, they will want to live a certain way. They do not work during the weekend and they watch films or sports matches during this time. The camp sustains itself through this authoritarian method. The reader is probably wondering how this camp differs from the world as we know it? It does not and that is my point. The world as we know it is the concentration camp, but instead of calling it tyranny or oppression, we call it life and when you call something "life," people will adopt it more readily. People cannot see that they are slaves, but this form of captivity is called "life" by economists, philosophers, doctors, poets, the powers that be etc. and thereby extoled and hence adopted. We are so hardwired on the system we cannot see it as a system. Instead it becomes part and parcel of "living."

Two fears strike the heart of the young impressionable conformist: One, they fear missing out on life by not conforming and two, they are afraid of what people will think of them should they choose to deviate from the chosen path.

The system thrives on stigma. You stigmatize solitude, psychiatric illness, homelessness etc. What this does is induce the individual to conform.

It is not that you wouldn't enjoy solitude; it's that you are afraid you might enjoy it.

A common trait I see amongst entrepreneurs is that they delayed conforming until they had financially secured their future. What I mean is that rather than conform from their late teens and early twenties, they decided to work really hard in that time, build up their empire and then in their early thirties, they would settle down into marriage and so on, when they were financially secure. In contrast the textbook conformist conforms from a young working age and thus ends up paying off a mortgage for many years.

Being biased is the first mistake in the search for truth and those who conform are inherently biased.

The police govern those who break the law. Society itself governs those who defy conformity. Society is the police; it is the army; it is the government. Anyone who defies the system of conformity gets ridiculed. Through labelling society enforces societies will upon society. It is easy to blame the government; the true reality is that you should blame your best friends. It is they and not the government that decide how you live.

We think we are deciding the economic system when it is the economic system that decides us.

Kim Kardashian does not behave as she does to impress the government. She behaves as she does to impress her fans. Her fans regulate how she behaves. Now apply that same proposition to the average-not-famous individual. Who regulates how they behave? It is their family, friends, neighbours, co-workers etc.

The childhood classroom is where society is decided.

In the free world, society is the authoritarian government.

Man is trivial for he neglects the better part of his life for some future ideal and thus ends up misusing most of his life on a dream. Being happy in the future starts with being happy now.

We have been so poisoned with what lack of freedom entails in imprisonment that we come to regard being free as the world we live in. The reality is that despite the lack of enclosed walls we are prisoners to money, labelling, conformity and other things. We are prisoners to the economic system, and it would take intelligent life from another planet to point that out to us.

Your life has been decided from a noticeably young age.

There is no journey to happiness. Happiness is the journey.

To be unhappy because you are not living this dream life is the greatest insult to the universe.

What happened to the young child in school who decided to go against the grain? They got laughed at, demeaned and possibly bullied.

When a couple of people do it, it is a cult; when billions do it, it is life.

I see this with people who buy the lotto. They cannot see the billions of others who do the very same, all thinking they have a chance of winning it. Likewise, we cannot see the billions of others who conform that keep the system functioning. We think we are special; we are not; we are no better than the ants that serve the queen.

It has been long decided how you will live before you actually live.

So many in the free world commit suicide not because of depression but because of the depression caused by the economic system enforced on them.

You can be married and working and be existentially mature. It is much harder because you are embroiled in aspects of life that attract anxiety.

For some reason, the male of society is allotted more freedom. They can be more adventurous, daring, promiscuous, violent etc.

If the current system is so good, why do lawyers and psychologists make fortunes?

The individual will struggle to not be overwhelmed by the tribe but in the current system 90% of jobs involve liaising with other people and thus the influence of the tribe is a given and as such conformity is a by-product.

Imagine if intelligent life visited our planet. They would be aghast at how unhappy we are despite our dominance.

Are the people deciding the economic system or is the economic system deciding the people? I believe it is as much the latter as it is the former. People naively think that they are choosing to fall in love and have children. The true reality is that they are told to do this by the economic system. This whole "free choice" is implanted in their minds from a young age, that they are marrying and raising a family because they fundamentally choose to, devoid of any societal and economic influence. This is false. Everything, particularly in capitalist countries, is designed to manipulate you into believing that you are conforming because of free choice, when you are not.

One of the differences between communism and capitalism is under communism, the individual knows they are being told how to live. Both systems tell you how to live, but with capitalism, you are not aware of this.

Isn't it ironic if not tragic that the prisoners in a maximum-security prison are more secure in their existence than the free peoples of this earth! What do the prisoners worry about? Nothing, bar their release date maybe. What do the free people worry about? Everything! Image, money, relationships, friends, bills, death, boredom etc. Often, I think it is much better to be in chains than it is to be free. In some ways, the free world is the penitentiary.

One must reconcile the necessity of the system with its failure, chiefly the dread that accompanies one as they live day to day in the system. So many are doomed because the only see one way, one path by which to live their life and it becomes second nature to them. They either must conform or at least they suffer trying. The reality is that there are other paths to choose. But so many through the effects of education and our peers are hardwired on the system that they are blind to any other path.

One huge issue is the sexualisation of the individual. Everywhere they look people are telling them to have sex. It thus becomes entrenched in their unconscious mind that they need to be sexual and engage in sex. They thus become condemned to be sexual and this has a huge bearing on the need to conform.

If you try to avoid interaction, something which is seen as the cornerstone of human existence, you can only ever be a victim. All crime is a derivative of interaction. No interaction equates to no crime.

The coincidence is beautiful; what benefits the individual also benefits the economic system. Getting married and having children; working; supporting a sports team; going on two holidays a year. The economic system has taught us how to live, and hence be happy and furthermore it has brainwashed us to believe that we are not brainwashed. The economic system does not teach one to be grateful because gratitude does not benefit the said system as much as desperation.

You cannot trust a man who does not believe he is capable of murder.

Social media only makes people more afraid. It only makes them conform more. Not alone do we have friends, family and co-workers telling us how to behave; we also have people we don't know on social media telling us how we should behave. The more your identity is known by the tribe, the more you will be duped into conforming.

How many men and women follow these Instagram models? Millions. What do these men and women say to themselves when they idolize these social media icons? They say, "if only I had what they had, then I would be happy." "If only I was as good looking as that woman, I would be happy." "If only I was as successful as that man, I would be happy." They are in "I need" mode and that is why they suffer. This is what social psychologists call Social Comparison Theory. We are always comparing ourselves to other people and this makes us insecure.

The threat is psychological and not physical. But due to our socialization when young we become programmed to interact with people. We cannot see how they injure our esteem. We cannot see how we respond unconsciously to vindicate them.

An individual may fear another human physically, but they fear their own peerage psychologically. Assault is not our gravest concern; being laughed at is.

Conformity is an institution of fear.

Women have it tough such is the pressure to be the model woman. If the individual wishes to be more secure in their existence, they must distance themselves from social media, friends, parents and co-workers. All in all, to be fully secure one must turn away from the herd.

Imagine if the government said that all men and women were to be married by thirty and have three kids by forty, society would reject it outright. They would rebel against the tyranny. But you latently suggest it through calling it life and furthermore you make them feel guilty and shame about missing out on marriage and parenthood and they will adopt the system quite astonishingly with ease. But there is no difference in the two systems other than the method used to encourage them to conform. Both are concentration camps: One is called oppression; the other is called life. And because they are so brainwashed through education and the herd, they cannot see it as a concentration camp.

A shadow of the herd can never be free.

When the cult is religious, like Scientology, we question it; when the cult is violent, like criminal gangs, we question it; when the cult is political, like the fascists, we question it; but when the cult is economic, we just accept it.

Existence —— Expose Identity —— Become Labelled —— Anxiety —— Conform

Fig 6: *Anxiety is the mother of conformity. We are afraid of being labelled, yet condemned due to the economic system to expose our identity to the world. To neutralize this anxiety, we instinctively and unconsciously conform. Conformity is the unconscious response to being labelled.*

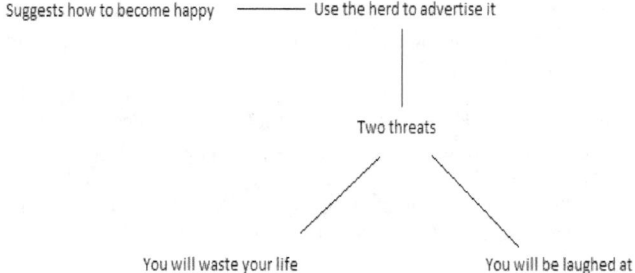

Fig 7: *To sum it up. What the system does is it suggests how we become happy. We see everyone else getting married and having children and consequently we come to believe we need the same to become happy. It then implements this through society itself. It gets parents, friends, neighbours, co-workers, teachers, doctors, celebrities, books, films, music etc. to compel us into mimicking the herd. This is then enforced through the two threats: A) we will waste our life should we not conform (as in we will waste our life if we do not get married and have children) and B) we will be laughed at by the herd.*

Narcissism

"The main condition for the achievement of love is the overcoming of one's narcissism." - Erich Fromm.

Narcissism is endemic in the capitalist condition. It is a direct product of the individual being labelled in the capitalist environment.

In order for people to survive in a highly stressful environment they must adopt a narcissistic façade. They do so to be labelled correctly.

This endeavours to harbour men and women who know nothing other than self-obsession.

Everything is about image to the narcissist. He works, marries and lives purely to uphold his projection to the world. He convinces himself in the mould of bad faith that he is happy through conforming. He cannot envisage any other existence other than conforming because that is how he claims applause off his peerage. This is an individual who is deeply insecure about being labelled.

In a sense the narcissist lives an inauthentic existence. They conform to earn approval and not because they gain pleasure from doing so. They exist under false pretences. They must become a husband/wife or father/mother so that they can procure respect from the herd. As such they play roles much like an actor in a film does. They are not living authentic lives.

They then pretend to be happy. They have been indoctrinated from youth to believe that happiness is obtained through conforming and as such they maintain the façade for the duration of their existence. They engage in Pretence Happiness. They feign happiness because this is how you are supposed to be happy.

This is the consumerization of life that taunts the narcissist. He or she chases marriage and work purely so they can be labelled correctly and not because they genuinely enjoy these things. In order to sustain the economic system, we have given birth to a culture of narcissism.

"It is not love that should be depicted as blind, but self-love." - Voltaire

The narcissist is obsessed with image. It terrorizes his daily existence.

---How will they see me?

---How will this mix with the majority?

---Will my friends and family approve?

The narcissism is also a product of a harsh environment where confidence and articulation are the required skills. The narcissist front serves as a template to survive in a world where attacks and stresses are frequent.

Insecure people want to be rich, beautiful and successful; they want the dream partner, the dream job and the dream life. There is a word that sums up this mentality: Narcissism.

Gratitude and narcissism are mutually exclusive. They are at the opposite ends of the spectrum. The more narcissistic you are, the less gratitude you convey; likewise, the more grateful you are, the less narcissistic you become.

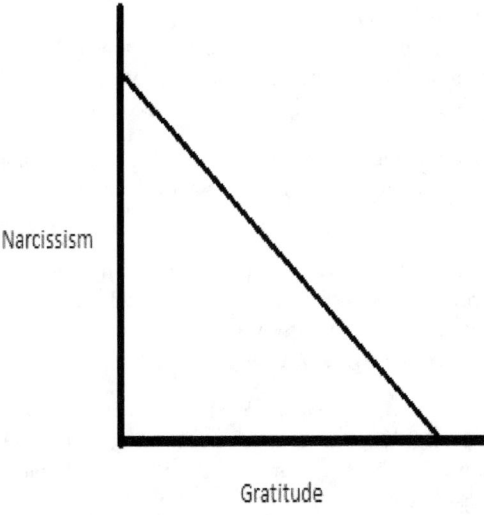

Fig 8: *As narcissism increases, gratitude decreases; as gratitude increases, narcissism decreases.*

Narcissism is just a nicer term for immaturity and insecurity. One in ten are full blown narcissists. But how many people display basic narcissistic traits? The answer is lots of people and it is created by the economic system they grow up in. The economic system tells them they have to be married and working the esteemed career and because they convey basic narcissism, they are condemned to do these things. They know of no other means to live. The universe may as well not exist for them because life is work and relationships. Their Economic Narcissism blinds them to the true realities of this world.

Narcissism is toxic. The individual sees others not as humans but as objects. He treats them as commodities into which he can gain in the world. The narcissist demands more always and threatens to leave if his or her demands are not met.

"Wealth consists not in having great possessions, but in having few wants."
- Epictetus.

The reason so many narcissists are observed in the capitalist economies is because they grew up with narcissistic parents and because life necessitates that they be narcissistic. Confidence is expected in society. The narcissist is insecure by default and adopts the persona to survive. It is a cosmetic confidence.

A huge reason why so many people mature in an insecure method is because they were forcibly educated when young. The system is not without its flaws.

The narcissist derides weakness. He deplores those whom he considers foolish or unsuccessful and often attacks them verbally. This apprehension towards weakness also manifests itself in his own soul. He cannot tolerate himself being observed as weak or easy.

The narcissist is to be avoided. His love is false; his feeling is a placebo; his kindness is reptilian. Often, they change once they marry for their unconscious realization that they now own the other individual serves to bring out the beast in them.

There is a faint hint of narcissism in us all and more than people cater for. We want to be admired by society and this urge, along with the need to supress the boredom steers our daily exchanges.

Look at those Instagram models. They think that because they have a million followers or likes, that everyone loves them. They then think they are happy. But they are not. It is an extortionate happiness, if such a thing exists, because they need people to like them in order to like themselves.

"When people like me, then I will like myself." There is a word for such a mentality, and it is called narcissism. "Why is it that people seek recognition from others? In many cases, it is due to the influence of reward-and-punishment education." - Ichiro Kishimi.

It is quite easy to be narcissistic within society; in contrast, it is exceedingly difficult to be grateful within the same society.

We are the only animal for whom existence is not enough. Any other animal, once they are fed, warm and have shelter, they are happy. This is not the case with humans. We need sex, we need to earn money, we need to be loved, we need people to like us and so on.

There may be eight billion humans living on planet earth, but you will not find another one in a thousand billion galaxies in the rest of the universe. This is where I diverge from Frankl's philosophy. He remarked one needed meaning in life. But if your meaning is governed by narcissism, you will suffer, rather than find fulfilment. Secondly, should your meaning fail to provide substance, one should in my view always have gratitude to fall back on. You may lose your job, your relationship may disintegrate, your football team might lose, the film you watch may be of poor quality. But you should always have gratitude to lean on. That you are alive in this universe is cause for celebration regardless of whether you are succeeding or failing.

We can learn so much from animals. There is not an animal alive, outside of human beings, that worries about not being liked. Likewise, there is no animal, other than humans, that gets anxious about the question of meaning. There is only one insecure animal on this whole planet and that is man.

The whole premise of beauty is that you want to be liked in order to like yourself. That is why one is infatuated with sexual attractiveness. They want to be liked and that is why they are unhappy. The same applies to this dream life. We want a nice house, a fast car, expensive clothes and so on, so that when people admire us, we again feel good about ourselves. This is a disease. This material happiness is why people are ironically unhappy. Kill it.

Narcissism is difficult to treat for it involves the individual acknowledging his own problem, which is considered feeble in the eyes of the narcissist.

We are still animals and yet to be called an animal would be an insult. That is the ego of man (particularly the narcissist). He believes that because he can speak, walk, build skyscrapers, see into the atom and much more that this planet is his entitlement.

Jealousy is a glaring sign of insecurity.

The narcissist is obsessed with two things: A) Seeking validation off people and B) Comparing him or herself to other people. As such they live insecure chaotic lives.

"People want to have purpose and meaning in another's lives, but ultimately they must come to realize that they cannot depend on others for validation, and with that realization they finally acknowledge and understand that they are fundamentally alone." - Irvin Yalom.

Taking things personal is a sign of insecurity. Your self-esteem should in no way be related to how others interpret you. Whether they approve of you or not, should be irrelevant. One must overcome their Labelling Anxiety.

The quest to be beautiful or remain beautiful is a response to labelling. You obsess over beauty because you want to be seen (be labelled) beautiful. It is naïve to think that this is determined by the individual and the individual alone; it is actually determined by society through being known, which then determines the individual. When you expose society to society, this determines the individual through labelling.

Validation must come from within and not from other people.

There is a hunger to fall in love which is healthy; but there is a desperation to fall in love which is insecurity. This is particularly the case with the narcissist. They yearn to "fall in love," purely to appease the tribe.

Generally, those who are desperate to fall in love, do not fall in love. They are too self-doubting to do so. They are so in need of love that no one can love them. They want so much to be loved that they do not realize that one must give to otherwise receive it.

This disease associated with image is sickening. People do not live to make themselves happy. They live to make other people happy and in doing so they become happy. This is typical of the narcissist. This whole idea that you cannot like yourself until you are liked by another person is sickening. It is despite the age of technology and reasoning, one of the failures of humanity. "One reason why birds and horses are not unhappy is because they are not trying to impress other birds and horses." - Dale Carnegie

People can mistake Frankl's hunger for meaning for the hunt for gratification. With Mature Conformity people approach these things in an authentic method. But Immature Conformity, which is the result of narcissism, one yearns to be gratified through these things. The inauthentic person says: Once I have A, B, C and D, then I will be happy. This is the misuse of Frankl's philosophy. They find meaning through these things, but they are poisoned by narcissism.

Technology rather than unchaining man has embellished his narcissism.

The narcissistic snake tightens its coils around the vulnerable individual. Its venom tells them that in order to be happy they need to be loved or "in love.". The antidote to this capitalist narcissism is to teach them to love their existence in this universe. When they do this, they convey gratitude, they mature and hence open themselves up to being loved.

Nobody thinks in terms of atoms or cells or organs. They look in the mirror and do not see these things. They see their face, which is an illusion, that instils a belief within them that they of are worth.

The capitalist narcissistic parasite infects us in adolescence. We compute we need a relationship not because we enjoy it but because we need to be seen in one. This is the consumerism of love. This is already a bad start for the individual. Secondly the actual substance of this love is predictable. We look for someone who when we are seen with them, will impress the tribe. More consumerism. We then proclaim this is love when it is not. It is convenience. It is a marriage borne out of infantile fear. And the true tragedy of this consumeristic love is that we do not see it until we grow old.

The reality is one should be happy with nothing, that is if they are truly mature. If they are not it is usually because of narcissism that has infected them since youth.

You cannot be mature if you are narcissistic; you cannot be secure if you are narcissistic; you cannot be free if you are narcissistic. Narcissism is the number one enemy of being happy.

Narcissism and capitalism are like a devoted husband and wife.

The good thing about the Labelling Anxiety is that it makes people moral. The bad element to it, is that it makes people insecure or worse, narcissistic.

Unhappiness benefits the system more than happiness; insecurity is more beneficial than maturity; gratification is more addictive than gratitude.

Man is the only animal that can hate himself; he is the only insecure animal; he is the only animal that can stare into the mirror and see shame staring right back.

To the insecure narcissist, happiness is material, it is consumption, it is success, it is image, it is sex, it is greed.

"We seldom think of what we have, but always of what we lack." - Arthur Schopenhauer

The insecure are desperate to be labelled correctly and this desperation is not healthy and ultimately prevents them from ever being happy. Doing anything because you wish to be seen doing it, is the wrong reason for doing it. That is immaturity where one lives-for-others rather than lives-for-oneself.

Living-for-others is when you marry to be seen married. Living-for-others is when you live for the positive label of another person or persons. Think of the stereotypical narcissist: "I will be rich, beautiful, smart, funny and confident, all so people can see me as such." They are motivated by procuring a positive label from society.

Living-for-others is narcissism, pure and simple. If you live-for-others you will never become happy. You have to live-for-oneself and you do this by being grateful for being alive.

Education has one huge negative and that is we become submissive to the herd. We live-for-others rather than live-for-oneself. Happiness is making the herd be impressed with us and this leads to much anxiety.

There is a difference between living for others and living-for-others. "Living for others," is where you live to help people or animals. Such as a homeless charity or an animal rescue. "Living-for-others," is where you build your life around the narcissistic template because you must be seen living such a template. Such a person lives to procure endorsement from individuals or perhaps society.

I do not see any resolution to this conflict. The economic system must change before man can change.

Such is the pressure on the individual to meet all these targets in order to be "happy," you would swear that a loaded gun is pressed against their forehead. This figurative loaded gun is actually the opinion of their peerage.

Basic narcissism is still narcissism and it is a huge source of unhappiness in people. Overcoming narcissism can lead to a better quality of life.

Look at mass murderers and you will see pattern. One of the similarities is low self-esteem. A guy asked out a girl and she laughed at him and a couple of months later he shoots a few people dead to get revenge on life's mistreatment of him. This is narcissism.

The poor man struggles to survive but the rich man struggles to live.

An example of the narcissistic eagerness is in our need to buy designer clothes. We need to be seen with the label. We are afraid to be seen without the label. Now one must transfer this insecurity into other aspects of life. Such a person needs the job, the marriage, the family etc. because they need to be labelled accurately. Such an individual is deeply polluted by narcissism.

"A man's worth is no greater than the worth of his ambitions." – Marcus Aurelius. If your philosophy (your ambitions) in life is flawed, then as a human you will be flawed also. Take your gratification and turn it into gratitude.

The narcissist is tainted with fear. That is their predominant emotion. They seek this designer life because ultimately they are afraid of what people will think of them. The mature person in contrast recognises the various choices in life and picks the one that gives the most pleasure. They are content to marry but they would also be happy alone.

Trying to make people like you should be classified a psychiatric illness.

The Hedonic Treadmill concept is one of narcissism. Such a person must keep moving forward in order to feel good about themselves. They must keep succeeding to be gratified and in order to stay gratified (stay on the same spot of the treadmill) they must keep succeeding.

Instead of ushering the students straight from school into college we should give them a break. We should let them find themselves. We should enable them to discover the world and in doing that they may just discover themselves.

It is easy to recognise the addiction to alcohol or drugs or gambling. But what of the addiction to status? What of the addiction to being labelled correctly? This is an addiction that haunts the narcissist.

"He who has a why to live for can bear almost any how," said Nietzsche. But your why must not be corrupted by narcissism. If your why is narcissistic, you will not become happy.

Narcissistic friendship much like narcissistic love, is toxic to one's maturity.

We fear being known by ourselves, as much as by another person. The mirror is often our adjudicator, in the same vein as the eyes of our peers are. You wonder why males or females must have their hair cut a certain length, yes, to appease their peers, but also to appease themselves. In a sense we are cut off from ourselves. There is a split. There is a demon residing in our souls, our conscience, much like Iago, telling us how we must behave. This demon is called narcissism and one must purge it in order to become happy within themselves.

Those who are narcissistic, consist of two people. There is a monster inside them, telling them how to behave. How to act, how to dress, how to be approved and so on. They do what the monster says and they feel gratified. But they are still sick.

There is a split in the mind of the narcissist. They either love themselves or they hate themselves. You can just imagine such a person standing in front of the mirror saying to themselves: If only I was richer, if only I was more attractive, if only I was more successful; then I would be happy. I see some on forums and they are their own worst enemies. They think people slander them, when the reality is they slander themselves. The demons of this world reside in their conscience. They are still in the adolescent narcissistic phase of maturity, where they must be loved in order to love themselves. I recall a man wallowing in self-loathing and self-pity over the fact that every time he socialized with his mates, they all managed to seduce a woman, yet he failed. This man has no enemies in life bar himself and unless he overcomes his inherent narcissism, he will remain unhappy for the rest of his life.

Man, fears being nothing as much as being evil.

What you should look for in a person be they a friend or partner is maturity and not confidence. The immature individual who adopts a narcissistic façade will display confidence and this can deceive you.

The narcissist much like the schizophrenic has an impaired awareness. He or she doesn't realize they are a narcissist.

We don't have a rape culture; we have a narcissistic culture. And with narcissism accompanies entitlement and with entitlement accompanies violence.

There are independent women out there, no question. But then there are narcissistic women who need to get married to be fashionable. And the same applies to men. These people are immature.

Image is like a drug to the somatic narcissistic female and because of this she becomes obsessed with true love, relationships, vanity etc.

Does the narcissist see the universe or the kidneys and liver in his/her body or do they understand the quantum theory of the atom? No. Existence to the standard narcissist is marriage and money. The earth may as well be flat, and the stars may as well not exist because the narcissist does not acknowledge them.

There are far more narcissistic people than we cater for. There are so many that its almost not even a personality disorder anymore. It is seen as a clique.

The somatic narcissist is corrupted by status. How does he or she portray a pristine image to society? He or she constructs their whole life in such a way that people will be impressed by them. So, they need the correct car, clothes, body and so on. One other thing they need is the correct partner.

If the culture is narcissistic, then you will be narcissistic, and you cannot be happy with narcissism. You get emotionally gratified, yes, but never a concrete happiness. By culture, I mean your parents, friends, neighbours, co-workers, celebrities, politicians etc. When you immerse yourself in narcissism, you become a narcissist, be it basic or full blown. A prime example of this is a group of narcissistic friends, be they male or female. They all put each other under pressure to behave the same way and want the same things. They are all individually afraid of the collective. Take a group of young females for example: They all must look attractive, wear expensive clothes, they all need to be in a relationship and so on. Basically, they all must behave as the standard "woman" should behave. They are all in effect corrupted by each other and the only way to get out of it and hence become mature is to extract yourself from the said group. But I repeat, if you are narcissistic, you cannot be happy.

In order to be grateful, one must overcome narcissism; in order to love, one must overcome narcissism; in order to live, one must overcome narcissism. Narcissism is the enemy of happiness.

The narcissistic individual with low self-esteem yearns to be loved. There is alas no such thing as being in love or being loved. Love is something you must cultivate together. It is not a feeling or sensation; it is a profession.

The narcissist prostitutes his identity to society. The narcissist is society's prostitute. This obsession with presenting a certain image is prostitution, be it male or female. You are just pawning yourself if you depend on presenting a certain image to society, so that they will be "impressed" by you when they observe you. You are just trying to make yourself as attractive as possible so people will like you and perhaps you can earn money from the fact that they like you, be it male or female. The Instagram models are really just prostitutes, that pawn their image for popularity.

If your whole existence revolves around procuring endorsement from the observing herd, you are no better than a prostitute.

Narcissists are societies prostitutes. For endorsement they exchange individuality.

A good deal of your time in this universe will be spent unhappy if you are absorbed in making people like you.

A woman I read about, spends most of her time thinking about how much she hates her thighs. She can give you a detailed report on what is wrong with them. She forgets all the places those legs have taken her, all the miles they have walked for her.

"Vanity and narcissism - the compulsive need to be admired and praised - undermine one's courage, for one then fights on someone else's conviction rather than one's own." - Rollo May

Beauty is fleeting; your attitude lasts till the day you die.

It is not a fundamental constant of nature that you need to be married or in a relationship. You feel this way because in part the system is enforced on you. You hear and see so much propaganda pertaining towards love and relationships that you instinctively come to believe that you need to be in one. This is what Mere Exposure Theory says.

With gratification there exists no top of the mountain because the mountain keeps getting higher. No matter how much you earn or receive, you never become happy, you just want more.

To counter being gossiped about, we try to make other people jealous of us. This is most certainly the case of the insecure and immature individual. They are petrified of being thought of negatively and thus resolve to live in such a way to make people jealous of them. So, a male may seek out the most attractive woman to be his partner, just to show off his life to the people who bullied him when young. Or a woman will spend 80,000 dollars on plastic surgery to make her more attractive because she was considered "ugly" prior to the surgery. The opposite to gossip, for the immature individual, is not happiness, but rather envy.

Comparing yourself to others is linked to your obsession with being liked in order to be happy. You attest that if only you had what this other person had, then you would be liked and hence happy. Again, it is narcissism attacking your conscience.

Commoditized happiness: When you "look happy," you feel happy. It is linked to labelling in that one wishes or desires to be labelled appropriately.

"When man discovered the mirror, he began to lose his soul." - Emile Durkheim.

It is only human, to want to be liked. To become a man or woman, one must overcome this desire.

The illusion of life spawned by the economic narcissistic cult inflicted on the child when young blinds them to the true realities of this universe. If they could only see the universe, they would not be as narcissistic.

Generation Narcissist: That is the world we live in.

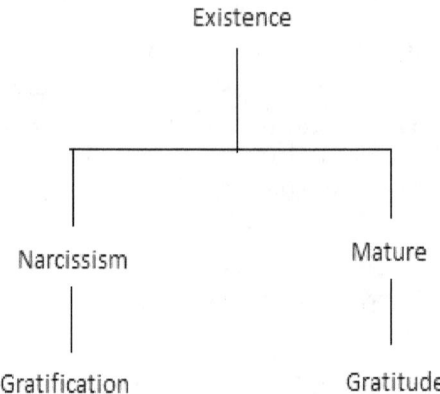

Fig 9: *Narcissism leads to Immature Conformity which leads to one addicted to being gratified. The correct attitude to have is to be mature which leads to gratitude.*

Look at the average football fan. In order to feel gratified his team must win. It is an addiction, just like one becomes addicted to heroin. Now one must apply this to everyone else. A woman must buy the specific dress, again in order to be gratified. Then the high wears off like a drug and she must buy a new one the following week in order to be gratified again. This is narcissistic gratification and the way to counter it is to just be grateful for being alive in this universe.

Suffering is not just caused by pain but also desire.

This is the one negative of American culture and there are many terrific elements of American culture, but this capitalistic narcissism is revolting to look at. A lot of these mass murderers in America are the product of narcissism. I would suggest that in order to solve their problems with gun culture, they should first start with Generation Narcissist. The irony of it all is that this narcissistic culture is worth trillions to the American economy.

Some feminist authors get a hard time for commenting on rape culture. They get attacked for criticizing men when the reality is, they are criticizing narcissistic men who are pulverised by entitlement. Statistically a lot of these men who commit sexual assault or rape have elements of narcissism to them.

The narcissistic relationship is one of gratification. They must keep moving forward, keep improving and keep succeeding for the relationship to survive. One of the characteristics of the authentic relationship is that they can say a lot without saying anything; they do so much without doing anything.

People have been educated from a young age through the Economic Narcissism that happiness entails doing A, B, C, D and E. Such immature narcissistic people need in order to "be happy", a fancy career, a fancy partner, a fancy house, a fancy car, a fancy appearance, fancy clothes, three fancy holidays a year etc. This is a narcissistic happiness. They have been taught that this is what "happiness" is. These are immature individuals.

What is good for society is not always good for the individual. Marriage is often an example of this.

Narcissism is when one bullies oneself.

We spend so much time trying to be coveted and that is why we are unhappy.

The full-blown narcissism is devoid in authentic love.

Image is the most tranquil opiate of the narcissist.

The national personality disorder of America is undoubtedly narcissism.

The narcissist is grossly immature and has not evolved. They are still in adolescence, consumed, coerced and cornered by image.

"Knowing yourself is the beginning of all wisdom." - Aristotle.

The naïve narcissist thinks: Once I conform, I will be happy. This is actually counter-productive for the paradox of success then kicks in and impedes them from being happy. The mature person remarks that they can be happy with nothing as much as everything.

Fifty years ago, in America it was paranoia. Now it is paranoia and narcissism.

Our eyes, the organ that gives so much, slowly strangle us.

The narcissist must do; the mature individual can do. The narcissist must buy designer clothes, must have a traditional wedding, must have a specific job, must be living in certain house etc. They must do all these things and more because they are fundamentally insecure about being labelled by society. They possess an intense Labelling Anxiety.

The narcissist is stricken with envy. He or she sees other people doing well and feels bitter. "I deserve a life as good as them." The narcissist too is just devoured by this dream life. Friends, a partner, a house, a good figure etc. They suffer an intense Capitalistic Insecurity, haunted by image and condemned by labels.

I knew a guy who changed his name and had plastic surgery, just to make women like him. This man would never become happy. He was too narcissistic to do so.

When you defy the system, you can overcome your narcissism.

The narcissist is afraid of being humiliated. Society tells him or her: You can't live alone, we will laugh at you; you can't be homosexual, we will laugh at you; you can't have psychiatric problems, we will laugh at you; you can't marry someone who is not of a good status, we will laugh at you. Essentially the narcissist is so afraid of being laughed at, that they conform out of fear. Now you must apply that apprehension to the elementary individual who is not a full-blown narcissist but shares some minute qualities. They too are afraid to be humiliated and as such their behaviour is defined by pleasing the tribe.

"What Orwell failed to predict was that we'd buy the cameras ourselves, and that our biggest fear would be that nobody was watching." - Keith Jensen.

You need less and not more to experience life.

Everyone displays elements of narcissism when young, ranging from basic to full-blown. Some grow out of it, but some do not.

The two most common words in the narcissistic dictionary are: I need. The narcissist says: "I cannot be happy until…." The mature person says: "I am happy despite….."

People are not afraid of solitude. They are afraid of being seen living in solitude.

When education is done right it produces maturity, gratitude and compassion. But when it is done wrong, it produces narcissism.

Narcissism and gratitude are mutually exclusive. Narcissists do not possess the maturity to be grateful and hence happy. Their happiness is tied to admiration. When they are admired, they feel gratified, but the high wears off and must be reclaimed. The pendulum swings between boredom and gratification.

A continuous source of woe is that you continuously compare yourself to others.

The capitalistic dream is often a Capitalistic Insecurity.

I would theorize that most people if not all go through a sort of narcissistic phase in adolescence and it is just a question of whether they can extract themselves from it as they grow older.

The narcissistic person treats life as if it were another person, designed to make them happy.

The universe does not care about you. For every one who makes it, fifty thousand must suffer. It is simple economics. This is the capitalist system wherein the minority control the wealth and the majority work to make the minority rich.

I would echo the sentiments of Rollo May to an extent: Implicit conformity is nothing more than cowardice. Such a person is afraid to be an individual.

The easiest way to be existentially mature is to see the universe. In contrast the insecure or narcissistic individual only sees life as love and work. To them the atoms in their body or the billions of stars in the milky way may as well not exist.

Name one other animal that has plastic surgery to make itself more attractive and hence feel good about itself. Name me one? It is basic narcissism: "When I am liked, then I will feel good about myself and hence, I will become happy. When people are impressed by me, then I will love myself." If that is your attitude, I am telling you, that you will waste a good deal of your life being unhappy.

The threat of being labelled is overcome by the addiction to conversation, the addiction to sex, the power of the herd and the power of image.

You can always tell the immature in that they value human life above that of all other animals.

The narcissistic woman dreams of her wedding day from the age of four.

The narcissistic male or female cannot even bear entertain the thought of not being married. This desperation does two things: A) It makes them insecure because they hunger defiantly to find love (and cannot be happy without it) and B) It malnourishes their actual marriage should they get one. The irony is tragic in that the narcissist is so desperate to be married by a certain age that they do not possess the adequate skills to be married.

You can learn so much about this world by analysing yourself.

Capitalistic Insecurity

"We are effectively destroying ourselves by violence masquerading as love." - RD Laing.

The Capitalistic Insecurity is a narcissistic insecurity.

One must ask themselves how people of the capitalistic persuasion can possess so much and still be unhappy or insecure. They may have a luxurious standard of living and yet they are tainted with hostility. The reason is because of what I term the Capitalistic Insecurity. For such a sufferer, it is not enough to have wealth and a comfortable standard of living, they must be popular, beautiful, respected etc. In other words, they wish to be labelled a precise way. These are people who need to be gratified each day in order to feel glad. They are blind to the universe and the chance that precedes existence.

They possess such an insecurity because they are inherently narcissistic in nature. They wish to be labelled correctly and when they are not, they wallow in despair.

One of the most common sources of unhappiness is the failure to meet the stipulations of conformity. The sufferer looks at other people who seem to have it all. They have the career and the relationship. Then when the sufferer looks at themselves, they see failure. What this conveys about those who suffer as such, is that they are still in the education phase of childhood. They have not matured as adults. They only feel good when the herd approves of them and that is the fulcrum of why they need a relationship to be happy because when they are in one, they unconsciously recognise that the herd validates them. They look good through the eyes of others and this derives from childhood education. This is the Capitalistic Insecurity. A mature adult simply does not care what the herd thinks of them, be they in a relationship or not.

The Capitalistic Insecurity manifests itself in so many ways. The sufferer needs to have friends, a partner, a job, needs to be confident, sexy and smart. What they do not realize is that they feel this way because society has told them to. Society has in a sense created them. It has chosen their dreams and unfortunately also their anxieties.

If one takes the decision theory of why one conforms, chiefly relationships, the individual does not account for the serious pressure they are under from society to conform. They do not realize that the very people they love (friends and family) are covertly telling them how to behave and what to achieve. Men and women alike are under severe duress to be the model man and woman. Just as one conforms to gender norms to be approved, one seeks out relationships or family because one wishes to pacify the herd. Now this urge is unconscious in its fabrication. Akin to when you drive your car, you stop at the traffic lights or put on your indicator or change gears unconsciously, you do all those things on instinct because that is how you have been taught.

To paraphrase Plato: You can forgive a child for being naïve about life; the true tragedy is when you have adults who are still childlike. This is the Capitalistic Insecurity. These so-called adults are still in adolescence.

"If you are lonely when alone, you are in bad company." - Jean-Paul Sartre.

This insecurity takes hold in adolescence. The males want to be wanted by the females and the females by the males. When they are rejected, they blame themselves for their failure to be desired. They experience anxiety and depression as a result. There are two ways to overcome this defective mindset: A) You become attractive. So, you spend money on plastic surgery and so on. B) You change the way you think. In other words, you do not measure your self-esteem in being wanted.

To found your security on your looks is to be insecure. To be obsessed with physical attractiveness is the most basic form of insecurity. You are obsessed with how you look because you want people to endorse you. Ergo, you are dependent on other people to like you in order to like yourself. In two words that is the Capitalistic Insecurity.

"As long as you still experience the stars as something above you, you still lack a viewpoint of knowledge." – Friedrich Nietzsche.

When we see everyone else doing it, we get it into our heads that this is the way things work. This is the power of Normative Social Influence. We become normalized on it. So, what does the young impressionable individual see? They see everyone working, marrying, having children, living certain established lives and so on. They become used to it. It becomes second nature. Just as they cannot perceive the nihilistic universe because they are taught not to.

There is a terror that afflicts the average people of society and it is called shame. They are afraid to walk into their parent's house unemployed. They are afraid to meet up with friends and exclaim they are partner-less. The fear of being laughed at motivates them and I emphasize the word "fear."

Analyse the famous person: They are so afraid that if they do not get a husband or wife, they will be laughed at by the viewing public. Now apply that simple fear to the ordinary person. Who are they afraid of? Parents, friends, neighbours, co-workers etc.

Man is the only animal who needs a solution for his existence.

In a sense the economic system has the sufferer drugged; work and relationships is the hallucination.

The next time you despair over looks, money, family problems, work problems etc. think of your worries relative to the universe. They mean something to the current economic system, but they mean absolutely nothing relative to the universe.

There is the friendship where you both accept each other for who you are and there is the friendship where you both determine each other for who you are.

It is those who embrace their condition, those who accept their failures, that live happy.

The entitlement of some people in this world is amazing. They expect the universe to unconditionally provide for them as if they are deserving of it. All we are is animals that can speak, that are living on a planet; we are entitled to nothing.

A woman once asked: "I am unattractive. How do I deal with this?" You deal with it by not tying your self-esteem to being desired. This woman is insecurity personified. She is still in the adolescence narcissistic phase of maturity where she must be loved in order to love herself.

It is your own choices, your own thoughts, that push you into the black hole and it is your own choices, your own thoughts, that can pull you back out.

"Do not spoil what you have by desiring what you have not." - Epicurus.

Man is the only animal that sells himself to the interpretation of another human.

I have sympathy for those who suffer from anxiety. I have no sympathy for those however who suffer from anxiety and keep doing the same things repeatedly expecting different results.

I still stand by what I have said in previous notes and I know most readers will not be happy with what I say. But you can be happy alone. In fact, it is the most secure form of contentment. The reason why so many refuse to be alone is not because they don't enjoy it, but because they fear the symbol of being a recluse. They are so afraid of being negatively interpreted by the herd that they conform implicitly to appease their peerage.

I see it on forums, men and women feel ashamed that they have never had sex or do not have a partner. Shame is a masterful influencer and in this case it implores people to conform, which in turn benefits the economic system. Why do these "ashamed" people think like this? They do, not because it is inherently wrong, but because this is how they have been brought up. This is how they have been brainwashed.

Moments of madness can also be moments of clarity. Often in the darkness do you finally see.

We are all suffering even the person who has got it.

Advice such as: "Are you living or waiting to die?" can actually be poor advice because the individual then gets it into their heads that they have to "live," in order to live. This then makes them seek out certain careers, certain relationships, certain commodities and so on, so they can put to bed the fact that they are not "living." But this can often lead to unhappiness.

We medicate people but refuse to medicate the exact cause which is the economic system.

The powers that be want you to be an agent of gratification. They want you to leverage your happiness on image, marriage, commodities, friendships and careers etc. They want you to marry someone you do not love, work in a job you do not like and buy things you do not need. They want you to do this because this is how economies thrive. It is only when you add up all the insignificants that you get a significant world.

"Imagine a society that subjects people to conditions that make them terribly unhappy then gives them the drugs to take away their unhappiness. Science fiction, it is already happening to some extent in our own society. Instead of removing the conditions that make people depressed modern society gives them antidepressant drugs. In effect antidepressants are a means of modifying an individual's internal state in such a way as to enable him to tolerate social conditions that he would otherwise find intolerable." - Theodore Kaczynski

Do not yield to the pressure from family and friends.

RD Laing said the source of schizophrenia was the family. What one must deduce from this is that one is under so much unconscious burden from family and friends to meet targets. If one takes the decision theory of who you are and what you want, this pressure has a huge bearing in how you decide.

Eliot Rodgers was a man who had everything if you were looking from the outside in. He had money, was living in the dream country, was good looking etc. Why then did he kill six people and injure fourteen others? The answer is the Capitalistic Insecurity. Life had told him that in order to be of value, he had to have a beautiful woman by his side. He had to be working the esteemed career. If he was not doing these things, he was in the eyes of the American capitalistic culture, failing. It was not that he did not have enough. He had too much and did not appreciate what he had; he had too much and needed more. Now this exact same mentality afflicts billions across the world. People attest that they cannot be happy until they have X, Y and Z. It is a disease, but one that is the heartbeat of economies.

With freedom comes pressure. That is why so many commit suicide in capitalistic countries.

Stop thinking about how you need to be in love and working this dream career in order to be happy. Instead start thinking about how lucky you are to be alive in this universe. With regards the universe we are a speck of dust of inconsequential size. Negate what worries you; stop thinking about your dreams. Start coming to terms with this existential reality, which is that nothing truly matters. When you do that, you liberate or unburden yourself.

You are your own god and your own executioner; it is your own thoughts that make you who you are.

Every animal on this planet has it bad except one: Man. We do not realize how good we have it.

One atom does not make a human; nor does two. So why then does trillions upon trillions?

The fact that psychologists have employment demonstrates just how impulsive and unaware we are of ourselves. That we need another individual to indicate the flaws in our lives conveys that we are not self-analytical enough. We do not question ourselves enough and thus we cannot change ourselves. You can learn so much through virtue of analysing yourself.

Plastic surgery is not the answer; a psychologist is. A life with less can often equate to a life with more.

"Everybody in the world is seeking happiness—and there is one sure way to find it. That is by controlling your thoughts. Happiness doesn't depend on outward conditions. It depends on inner conditions." - Dale Carnegie

You do not want the day you die to be the same day you finally free yourself of anxiety and worry.

By far the biggest problem in capitalistic culture is low self-esteem. The sufferer is either not sociable enough, smart enough or sexy enough and maybe perhaps all three. These are simply different ways of saying they want to impress people to be happy. They tie their self-esteem to being endorsed by society. Their happiness is relative to how people interpret them. They then latch onto the physical/mental illness card as a means to justify why they are failing. This is self-pity rearing its ugly head. "It's not me, it's the illness." It comforts them and gives a sense of hope in that they assert that if they could only beat this mythical illness, life would suddenly fall into place. It will not though. It will not because their happiness is directly proportional to how people interpret them. At the heart of it this is the problem. People do not approve of them positively. Now this stems in part from education. That we were thrown into a pack of hyenas they call our peers shaped our wills and wants. Now there are two ways to counter this low self-esteem. One is to become sociable, smart and sexy. So, you get a life coach, you get a degree and you have plastic surgery all in the hope of being approved by your peers. The other solution is to change the way you think. Instead of tying your self-esteem to being endorsed, you tie it to the fact that you are alive in this universe. Instead of being so conscious of what people think of you, you do not care what they think of you.

We spend the better part of our lives trying to manufacture a better one.

Being obsessed with being approved is a drug just like heroin. It leads to addiction, which invariably leads to suffering. It is narcissism and in order to mature, this narcissism must be overcome.

When you see fame as the solution to your problems you are generally insecure.

Why don't you become an individual instead of becoming an ideology?

We are akin to the worker bees, devoid of freedom, condemned to serve the queen of economic growth. The current environment (economic system) makes people insecure and it does so from the moment we are collectively educated.

Self-esteem derived from either beauty or money is a precarious self-esteem.

The happiest people do not live in the richest countries. They live in the poorest countries because they measure success differently. They are not corrupted by this capitalist rat race. Happiness is to them just tending to a farm and being alive. Happiness to the capitalist is being perceived as popular through the eyes of others.

It is quite ironic in that the individual of a capitalist heritage possesses more wealth but less maturity.

Those who have life sussed out are the ones who can find comfort in the solitude. "In a culture in which interpersonal relationships are generally considered to provide the answer to every form of distress, it is sometimes difficult to persuade well-meaning helpers that solitude can be as therapeutic as emotional support." - Anthony Storr

The mature person grows out of the educational popularity contest; the immature person continues to embroil themselves within it.

We have all heard of the American Dream; but what of the American Reality? One of the failures of the American Dream is that we do not hear about all the people who did not make it.

One must ask why there is a correlation between the economic affluence of a country and its increase in narcissism. You would think it would be the opposite. That the better the economy would reduce those with narcissism. One must wonder why the happiest people come from the poorest parts of the world.

The Bandwagon Effect: That we see parents, friends, neighbours, co-workers, celebrities, politicians, teachers, doctors and so on, all getting married and starting families, we unconsciously get brainwashed into doing the same thing.

It kind of links to the Framing Effect in Behavioural Economics. Society puts a positive spin on getting married and working the esteemed job. The environment promises happiness by living such a way. You frame the dream life a certain way and people buy into it instinctively. They positively frame the good life as a means of becoming happy. They leave out all the stress and negative aspects of it.

Then you have Positive Framing with threats. The dream life is X, Y and Z, but if you don't do it, we will laugh at you and you will not experience life as you should. There are two threats: A) We will laugh at you (which is labelling) and B) You will waste your life.

"We are all alone, born alone, die alone, and - in spite of True Romance magazines - we shall all someday look back on our lives and see that, in spite of our company, we were alone the whole way. I do not say lonely - at least, not all the time - but essentially, and finally, alone. This is what makes your self-respect so important, and I don't see how you can respect yourself if you must look into the hearts and minds of others for your happiness." – Hunter S Thompson.

They say it takes courage to marry. It takes even more courage not the get married.

"I want happiness." Take away the I; that is ego. Take away the want; that is greed. All you are left with is happiness.

Do not ask how the world can make you better; ask how you can make the world better.

The successful man and the attractive woman put themselves under severe pressure to be sexual.

The dream life is very alluring. No one accounts for the risk involved. No one sees the struggle. They only see the happiness. So many are left stranded in their mid-life because the dream does not materialize as was planned.

I dreamt of a world where people were simply happy. They were happy not because they were rich or beautiful or funny or successful. No, they were happy simply because they were alive.

"There are more tears shed over answered prayers than unanswered ones." - Saint Teresa of Avila.

I see such and such individual, that are in their thirties, complaining that life has passed them by. Everyone else according to this individual has friends, families, are advancing in their careers and so on. This is symbolic of the Capitalistic Insecurity. Such a person conceives that they need X, Y and Z to be happy. They think like this because we have taught them to think like this. What they actually need to do is change their attitude.

The hard way to change your life is to physically change your life. The easy way is to change the way you think.

Imagine you were imprisoned on another planet and the dream was to escape to earth and make a home there. That is how you should approach life on earth as a human. That you are so blessed to be alive on this planet.

Viktor Frankl wrote such a good book in Mans Search for Meaning and it should be read by all. Now days, especially amongst the affluent, people are concerned about happiness as in man searches for how to be happy. The immature version of happiness is living the dream life. The mature version is gratitude.

The goal of life is to conceive of your own philosophy on how best to live your life. It may be through conformity or it may not.

I see on various internet forums, people talking about their "inadequate" mental health. They are depressed, anxious, worried etc. But they blame their minds. Not one person has ever blamed the economic system that causes their deterioration. That is how brainwashed they are on the system, that they blame themselves for what is the systems flaw.

The profitability of plastic surgery demonstrates how insecure people are. Plastic-surgery is a by-word for insecurity.

Rollo May attested that the deep-rooted problem with man was emptiness or apathy. I would disagree and I do not mean that in a negative way because Rollo May is a giant of existential psychology and a huge influence on these notes. But on the contrary, I see insecurity as the number one problem of westernized man and by man, I mean men and women alike. This Capitalistic Insecurity is almost like a sexually transmitted disease. Once it takes hold in youth, chiefly through education, it is so hard to rid the mind of it or even control it. The sufferer instinctively conceives that if they are not liked they are failing in life. The goal of these notes is to recalibrate your unconscious so that you no longer measure your self-happiness in terms of conforming.

"Very little is needed to make a happy life; it is all within yourself, in your way of thinking." - Marcus Aurelius.

The apocalypse would have to be imminent before man would truly cherish his existence.

Man is the only insecure animal.

The individual suffering the Capitalistic Insecurity does not find love. They are too insecure and too pressured to be "in love," the label, that they cannot discover love. They marry for fashionable reasons and not because the relationship has integrity.

By telling yourself that you must be in love or married by a certain age, you only distance yourself from actually being in love.

I wonder if love and the herd are mutually exclusive. Can we genuinely love someone in the shadow of the tribe? The point I am trying to make is that the mob has such an influence on who we choose to marry. I think to truly love, people must love in solitude. They must in a sense distance themselves from the tribe.

"Everything has been figured out, except how to live" - Jean-Paul Sartre.

So many tie self-esteem to sex and that is why they are unhappy.

The insecure capitalist child is used to getting everything they want. When they need a new phone or car, daddy provides. Unfortunately, the necessities change when they grow older. Now they need a relationship and a stellar career. Alas these things are much harder to accrue than a phone or car. When life fails to materialize as it should according to the capitalist doctrine, the individual despairs or worst, gets angry.

I recall a man remarking that part of the reason his marriage failed was because his wife kept saying that her sister had better things than she had. In other word's his wife's sister had a bigger house, a faster car, more children etc. This is systematic of the Capitalistic Insecurity. This woman (the wife) had so much and yet she was still painfully unhappy because life had taught her to be narcissistic. It had taught her that she had to out compete everyone else in order to be happy. Such a parent then teaches their children to be narcissistic themselves. The disease is self-sustaining.

The insecure capitalist is consumed by labels. They suffer an intense Labelling Anxiety. Everything becomes about being labelled appropriately. They buy a new phone worth 600 dollars or euros instead of a cheaper one because when seen with that certain brand of phone they get labelled positively. The same with clothes or other commodities. Now this exact mentality applies to love. They date or marry someone who enables them to be labelled appropriately. The relationship becomes commoditized.

There is so much more to existence than a clique. You must see life as a gift; if you don't, you are doing it wrong.

You can only be one of two people: Who you actually are or what society tells you to be.

We are so afraid of not being happy in our forties that we do not become happy in our forties.

In the dictatorship countries the government forces people to get married and have children. In the free countries of the west, it is the people themselves that force the people to get married and have children.

When the government tells the people, they revolt; when the people tell each other, they just accept it as true. Men and women, in the so-called free countries, look at retrospective men and women and then mimic them. They play a role of either a man or a woman. Society must rebel in a sense from society.

This narcissistic cult is then kept alive through their friends, who all put pressure on each other to conform to the diseased model.

Normality is subjective. It could be getting married; it could be living in solitude. The apprehensive individual however is so tarnished by the Capitalistic Insecurity that normal becomes the narcissistic template.

We must have the designer clothes, the designer house, the designer friends, the designer partner, the designer job. We live the designer life.

When we reach our thirties, we realize how immature we were in our teens. Likewise, we do not realize how unripe we were in our thirties until we are in our seventies.

It takes so much courage to be who you want to be.

Success is not money or marriage; success is reaching maturity in your twenties. Unfortunately, most people do not mature until their life is terminal. They will only learn how to live in the shadow of death.

I think we take being human for granted. I severely doubt an alien life form has produced a work of science/art as good as Albert Einstein's General Relativity. How many people understand that theory which governs daily existence as much as capitalism? It is the greatest achievement that mankind has ever produced, yet as we walk down a busy street at the weekend or meet friends, we are oblivious to it. We are more concerned as a species of this universe with physical attractiveness and the size of our bank balance. As a species we are blind. In order for civilization to function, people have lost the sense of what it takes to be human (the enormous chance) and it has been replaced by the question of what makes us human (material gain).

We need protection from the arsonists, the fraudsters, the rapists, the murders and the terrorists. But we also need protection from ourselves. It is our own wills and wants that retain us in a state of suffering.

Why are men and women obsessed with beauty from a young age? They are because we teach them to be, because we normalize sexual attractiveness within society.

Adolescents seem to have it all in capitalistic countries, but the sordid truth is they have truly little despite their wealth because they lack the most important skill of all: Self-assuredness.

Psychiatry will treat the disease (anxiety; schizophrenia) but not the cause of the disease. And what is the cause? It is family, education, work etc.

Children start off happy, thankfully, but then in adolescence, narcissism poisons them. It is in adolescence that they start saying "I need." I need to be loved; I need money; I need friends; I need a good job; I need that fancy car; I need to have sex. If only they could remain childlike in adulthood, they would be so much happier.

The insecure individual spends their life in fear. They suffer to find a viable partner and then when they find one, they suffer at the thought of losing him or her. It is violence masquerading as love.

It is a fact of life. The less people you depend on to be happy, the greater the chances of being happy. With regards true authentic friendship, less is more.

Years ago, before the dawn of the internet, the only critics were those paid to be critics. Now days, everyone is a critic. Thus, when one becomes famous, they are exposing themselves not to forty or fifty people, but to billions.

You make society fear each other and with this fear comes envy and with envy comes hate.

In our lust for success we slowly asphyxiate ourselves.

"You are only young once, but you can be immature forever." - Germaine Greer.

What I see that other people do not, is the fear of the herd that then motivates one to behave a certain manner. Take a group of friends. That they all know each other, they then all put each other under immense pressure to meet certain targets. They all must work and be in a relationship. They do these things in part to be positively labelled by each other. They corrupt each other and are corrupted by each other.

You may dislike the person you resent, but you don't fear them. Alas this is not so true for the people you admire. Your unconscious mind is in a constant state of panic with regards the people you like or love. You fear covertly losing their appreciation or respect and henceforth conform to placate their yearnings.

There was a documentary about a man who lived in a North Korean concentration camp and he escaped. He made an interesting point in that in the camp, despite the terrible conditions nobody killed themselves. Yet every day in Seoul (where he escaped to) he heard about someone who had committed suicide, despite their "liberty." It is indicative of what I am trying to demonstrate with these notes. You may be "free," but you still are in a state of anxiety. You worry about money, relationships, image, jobs etc. The other point and Viktor Frankl touched on this in his great book, that those in the concentration camp have hope, the hope that one day they will be set free. They may be under severe hardship, but they yearn for a day when they are liberated and such a thought enables them to soldier on. In contrast the very people we label free in today's world have no escape from their life of work and family. Once they take out a mortgage and have a family they are in a predicament. There is no higher calling or next level. They must continue to pay bills and care for the family and when they get stressed there is no avenue of escape. The honest individual is hence condemned to conform and tragically the only viable escape is often suicide.

The prisoner is enslaved by steel bars. The free person is paralysed by debt, image, morality and family.

The common man's woe is not existential in nature; it is ideological; it is economic based.

If you look at those murder-suicides that end up with families being killed, the reason why the husband/father or wife/mother commits such an atrocity is not existential in nature. It is due to the Capitalistic Insecurity. It is due to the economic system that enslaves people with debt, makes them work and consequently makes them so anxious about the future. Mankind despite the luxury we possess relative to our other species is still crippled with apprehension and that is the ultimate indictment of the current system.

We live in a world in which we are taught to seek protection from other people. But what if "other people" is yourself?

"The place to improve the world is first in one's own heart and head and hands, and then work outward from there." – Robert M Pirsig.

You try to physically force society to behave as you wish, they will revolt. But you plant in their minds the illusion of freedom and that by behaving this or that way, they will be both endorsed, and become happy and they will adopt it. This is how the economic system thrives. You tell people latently this is how you behave. You must be married, you must work, you must dress a certain way etc. You then make them anxious about failing to adhere to this model because you make them anxious about not being happy and with that fear accompanies their obedience.

When you corner people with a financial and psychological mortgage, they don't have time to think otherwise. As Noam Chomsky said: "People don't know what is happening and they also don't know that they don't know."

There are covert expectations or threats or perhaps both. From this stems your Labelling Anxiety, which can be neutralized by meeting these expectations. However, the individual who fails to meet them then gets devoured by the Capitalistic Insecurity and yearns for the day they do triumph in the mould of conformity.

The Labelling Anxiety influences all. In the immature, it has a huge bearing on why they conform to principles; in the mature it still has an influence but on a lesser scale.

The insecure individual does not want to be seen as a failure by their friends, family and co-workers and as such approaches life as if there is a loaded gun pointed at his or her forehead that forces them to conform. This loaded gun is actually opinion. Such an individual fear the very people they love. These people who must or have to conform are still in the adolescence narcissistic phase of maturity.

The heartbreak isn't that you aren't liked; the heartbreak is that you want to be liked.

Denial is truth. When people are in denial it's because they can't bear the truth.

People get counselling because they fail to get married. They should get counselling because they want to get married.

You can obtain an unlimited amount of happiness if you do two things: Learn to live in solitude and secondly, stop caring about what people think of you. With regards the second point, I remember reading (on the internet) about a woman who remarked that women should be paid more than men because it costs more to "upkeep" a woman. She argued for example that whenever she gets invited to a wedding, she must buy a new dress, get her hair done, buy makeup etc. which costs her a fortune. Then a commentator wryly remarked that she should just not go to the theoretical wedding, to which this woman responded: "If I don't go, the person who invited me, won't like me." In other word's the woman in question was afraid (and this applies equally to men). She was afraid of losing the friendship and this motivated her. In the same vein that if she does not groom and dress herself up nicely, guys will not like her. In the same vein if she does not marry and become a mother, her parents will see her as a failure. She ties herself esteem to being wanted, liked, approved or being desired. This fear shadows her every second of every day. She says to herself unconsciously: "If I don't do this, people will not like me." She and many others live day to day in complete utter unconscious fear. Thus (and this applies to men and women alike) if you just sever this adolescent need to be wanted, liked, approved or desired and trade it in for liking yourself in this secluded universe, you can gain a perpetual happiness. The woman in question would have more money, more time and most importantly more happiness if she just did not care what people thought of her. If she could just learn to be happy to exist, she could grasp an unlimited happiness.

If you were prepared to die for your country in a time of war, you would be classed as mature by the system. But you are not mature with respect to the universe, because you are basically sacrificing your life for an ideology. Likewise, if you are completely obsessed with being happy through work and relationships, the system again, says you are mature. But with respect to the universe you are not mature.

We are either regretting the past or dreaming of a warmer future. Either way, we neglect the present.

We are so inured on meeting people that it becomes second nature to us. We cannot see the apprehension in being known. What invariably happens is we become afraid of falling out with the people we do know, and this implores us to do things we do not wish to do in order to maintain the friendship (The Labelling Bind). It is the people we know that we fear. To be known is to be condemned and to be condemned is to be known. The true tragedy is that I see no end to the schism. Given the economic system we must work and so advertise our identity to the greater public and thus insecurity is certain. Then we have parents who are disappointed if we do not conform to the standardized male or female.

The people you hate provoke you; the people you love decide you.

Psychiatry says friendship, love and work, that is what is needed to be happy. They do not mention the fact that we come to fear the very people we depend on to be happy.

Your existence in this universe should be your ecstasy.

Do you know what we fear the most? It is not being beaten, raped or killed. It is being laughed at.

"If you are not having sex, you are missing out in life; if you are not married, you are wasting your life; if you don't have children, you are not experiencing life." The individual, such is their indoctrination, is "afraid of throwing their life away." This conformist guilt is a huge reason why people conform.

Nobody ever blames the system for their woes. It is their bank, their boss, their partner etc. but never the economic system.

Loneliness need not be your adversary. It can also be your salvation.

So good is the current economic system that we dread each day.

The average individual is more afraid of walking into their office than they are of walking down a war-ravaged street.

Anxiety is a psychological cancer.

To see things as a necessity is a position of insecurity. That is the difference between those who are miserable and those who are not.

Women need to be more existentially criminal to be more successful.

We should not blame the individual who conforms but rather the system that coerces them to conform.

You never see an abused dog wallow in pity. Despite its hardship, it sees itself as a survivor and not a victim.

The time to rebel is when the war is young.

I can guarantee these notes will fail because the system will sustain itself as long as we socialize with other people. People are social control. That they can label us means they dictate our behaviour. The trick to being truly liberated is to forgo the tribe.

We feel guilt letting down our parents. We feel guilt not being sexual. We feel guilt not meeting the demands of friends. This is it. We are so afraid to be an individual because we feel guilt. This conformist guilt is a huge incentive to conform.

In a thousand years' time, we will have found cures for cancer and colonized other planets in the universe. But I can guarantee the one thing that will still be the same as it is today, is that the individual will be subordinate to the herd. The economic system be it present or future is dependent on the individual being unconsciously afraid of the herd because when they are, they will conform to the principles of the herd.

In the authoritarian world we fear the government; in the free world we fear each other. In the concentration camp we commonly call life, our family are the government, our friends are the soldiers and our co-workers are the guards.

The insecure capitalist says: "I will become happy and then I will be grateful"; the mature individual says: "I am grateful" and therefore becomes happy.

The insecure vie for the dream life painlessly.

The average person lives 27,365 days. Not a lot. So, make everyone count.

When adolescent it was wrong to be homosexual, to have mental illness and to be a loner. This fear continues to haunt us as we grow older. Maturity is overcoming this fear of the herd.

It is no coincidence that old people learn how to live. Firstly, they are retired and thus not subject to the demands of the herd from a working point of view. Secondly and more importantly they are no longer deemed attractive looking and thus not absorbed in the dating game. Maturity is learning this when you are young.

I remember a plastic surgeon wryly remarking that he could do in one hour what would take a psychologist three-years. We are obsessed with appearance because when we look attractive people will like us and when people like us, we feel good about ourselves. We tie our self-esteem to being endorsed. This stems from childhood in that we tried when young to earn the approval of our peerage and in doing so we claimed a gratifying happiness. Maturity is overpowering this fear.

Everyone when finished school should go on welfare for a year or even two. They could teach themselves how to live by doing this. They could learn to live without money, they could learn to live by suffering, they could learn to live through rejection and being laughed at, they could learn to be happy with so little. Those things would stand to them for the rest of their lives.

If I were giving advice with regards finding someone to marry, I would strongly recommend you choose someone who is mature. Marrying someone who is desperate to be married so they can be seen married and part of the club, is not a healthy love.

We can see this apprehension with regards people who are diagnosed with serious mental illness such as schizophrenia. Parents of such an individual do not want other people to know. Why? They do not because they are afraid of what they will think of them. This is the fear. We are afraid of the opinions of people we know. Thus, it stands to reason that if you are not known, you cannot be hurt. But the economic system puts this to sleep. Within the current economic system (which includes education) we must socialize, and our minds instinctively learn that through conforming we can survive. But it is a precarious position to be in for every day is wave after wave of trying to either make people like us or maintain the fact that they like us. The ultimate failure of these notes is that I do not envisage any solution to this dilemma any time soon. The economic system of present is so embedded within the framework of society that revolution will never happen.

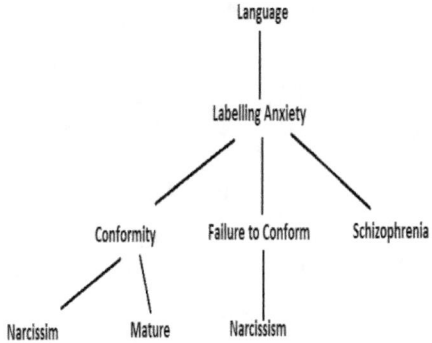

Fig 10: *From language stems our ability to label or be labelled. Hence a Labelling Anxiety is formed. From the Labelling Anxiety we either succeed in conforming or fail. The capitalistically insecure individual then either wallows in defeat or adopts a narcissistic approach to negate this insecurity.*

Chapter Two

Love

"I tore myself away from the safe comfort of certainties through my love for truth - and truth rewarded me." – Simone De Beauvoir.

(I wish to sincerely apologize for things I said in earlier versions regarding this chapter on love. In hindsight I was wrong to say these things. I was incorrect to state all sex is violence and I also regret discussing the bias towards love relative towards escorting.)

Love and the search for it is one of the biggest instinctive responses to the Labelling Anxiety. Condemned to expose our identity to the herd, we seek to neutralize the fall-out through being in a relationship (and other things). This is most certainly the case in the narcissistic individual who yearns to taste the mythical true love, purely so they can advertise a pristine image to the viewing public. Because of labelling they seek to conform. This is the Labelling Bind.

The immediate and instinctive response of the insecure narcissist is to be in a relationship. They think this way because life has taught them to think this way. Parents, friends and co-workers all say to the insecure individual that if they are not in a relationship, they are a failure.

Thus, the drive to find love becomes an obsession, purely so they can be labelled correctly. This is the commoditization of the relationship and their life. They are in a relationship to accrue a positive label from the viewing public. It is Bad Faith. It is inauthentic. Such an individual is so insecure that they cannot even dare contemplate a life without love and ultimately because of this obsession they lack the skills to make the relationship succeed.

Remember what I have already stated: where society is, the threat of stigma (the Labelling Anxiety) is. We are constantly being threatened with being stigmatized. This is particularly evident with respect to sex. Men can be labelled "perverts" and women can be labelled "whores." We thus, if we are moral, or even status conscious, try to avoid such labels. The means to do this is through love. Love is the method of having sex and being accepted at the same time. It is not stigmatized. I would estimate that about 50% of the reason why one desires to be in a relationship is because it is not stigmatized. But one is unaware of this. They are not cognizant that they gravitate towards love for labelling reasons.

I must confess that initially I believed (and wrote in earlier notes) that marriage benefited the female more than the male stigma-wise. I now consider this incorrect or at least incomplete. I initially remarked that stigma (slut shaming) funnelled women into relationships, but a similar stigma also applies to the male who has numerous sexual partners. He is labelled a sex pest or creep. This stigma leads to the threat of stigma towards other men, that funnels them, just like slut shaming does to a woman, into being in a relationship to have sex. Another way to think of it is if there is no equivalent stigma against men, why then does society continue to function? This is the eureka moment I had when walking my dog one day. You would think that if an equivalent stigma against men did not exist, fewer men would get married. The fact that society continues to exist, means that men must be marrying, which means there must be a retrospective threat of stigma guiding them to get married.

When it comes to sex, men are trying to have sex and avoid being labelled a pervert or creep. Likewise, with women, when it comes to sex, for they are trying to avoid being slut shamed. This is a huge percentage of why a relationship is so popular. It is a means to engage in sexual intercourse without being stigmatized (without being negatively labelled.)

The belief in true love conveys that one is narcissistic. True love is a symptom of narcissism be it basic or full-blown. Why should humans be able to taste true love and other animals cannot? Such an individual that believes in true love places man above all other animals; they forget that we are no better than the worms in the soil.

It says a lot about society that so many people believe in true love and the divine. These are people who can use reason and who we would not consider mentally ill. Yet they believe in true love and religion. This is how easily people are manipulated.

True love (not Authentic Love) is the most popular form of insanity. That we need external love in order to be happy should be classified a psychological disease. Do atoms have a soul mate? They do not. So why should trillions upon trillions of atoms that make up a human, have one? All we are is atoms.

Who or what is propagandizing the mind of the individual? It is not the government clamping their eyelids open and subjecting them to propaganda, like the protagonist in Stanley Kubrick's A Clockwork Orange. It is parents, teachers, doctors, celebrities, films, books, music and so on. All which show men and women finding "the one," falling in love with "the one" and having children with "the one."

True love is an acceptable form of psychosis. These infantile men and women attest that they cannot love their existence until they are loved by another. Thus, they spend large sums of money in trying to appear more desirable. This is the madness but because it is operated by most of society it becomes standardized as acceptable. "One man's faith is another man's delusion" - Anthony Storr

Following religions or football teams or famous people or even the person you love is not the problem. The focal point of the problem is why are people so easily manipulated to follow in the first place.

Men are blinded by their want to have sex; women are blinded by their want to feel loved. Both never realize the vocation of the universe.

The powers that be do not want smart solitary individuals who would advance mankind greatly. What they want is a society of addicts. They want people who are addicted to endorsement; who are addicted to sex; who are addicted to money. Why you may ask? They do so because that is the fuel of economies. "I don't want a nation of thinkers, I want a nation of workers." - John D Rockefeller.

What we call love is a subtle form of control. The man controls the woman and the woman vice versa; society controls them both.

The idea of the soulmate, that there is this one individual, this one animal that can speak who is designed to complete you, is as logically correct as the belief in god.

If men and women truly exercised their freedom, human civilization would be extinct in a hundred years' time.

The relationship you should work on is the one you have with yourself.

True Love is weakness.

Happiness tied to approval is a temporary happiness.

We are so hooked on finding this perfect person that we never find ourselves.

If schizophrenia afflicted 99/100 and love afflicted 1/100, then love would be the madness.

Young men and women are told by parents, told by friends, told by peers that if you want to be valued by society, be in a relationship. They fear a negative label should they choose to defy this.

Reality is the madness; it is the delusion. Men and women spending large sums of money in a desperate bid to be attractive is the insanity of our age. But because so many engage in this behaviour it is by psychiatry deemed conventional. When one person displays abnormal behaviour, it is madness; when society does it, it is considered a fashion.

True love is just something we have engineered through our ability to speak. We then get told when young that your purpose or at least one of them is to find this true love. We become so brainwashed that we believe what we are told. It becomes so familiar to us that being in a relationship becomes instinctive. We simply must be in one such is the brainwashing.

Love is not a necessity of the human condition. We can live without it. We can love our own solitude. When you were single, you were able to survive single. Imagine a world without love; men and women may finally be happy.

There is scarcely any love without any friendship.

I believe Authentic Love exists, but I reject the notion that it is our sole purpose on this planet.

Authentic Love makes people mature; narcissistic love makes people insecure.

You must mature to reap the rewards of Authentic Love and maturity is, paradoxically, being able to live alone. It is those who do not need love to be happy who are the ones that can be in love.

"To fully relate to another, one must relate to oneself. If we cannot embrace our own aloneness, we will simply use the other as a shield against isolation."- Irvin Yalom.

We are unhappy because we spend our lives trying to become happy in things that do not guarantee happiness.

If you think of two people in a relationship that have known each other since youth, their relationship is authentic, it is pure and it is not herd driven. These are two people who are together that is not by the desperation to please society. This is Authentic Love. Then think of two inauthentic people in their mid-thirties, who because of the fear of the herd, are so desperate to be married by a certain age, just so they can portray to that very herd that they are in a relationship. It is in a sense, a PR stunt. They are just in a relationship to procure endorsement. That relationship is narcissistic love.

Are you in a relationship because it makes you happy or because the symbol of the relationship makes you happy? Another way of putting it is this: Are you alive to make others happy or to make yourself happy?

An immature mind states: I need to be loved in order to love my life. A mature mind states: I love my life therefore I can be loved.

Observe yourself. How much time do you spend trying to fall in love? Now if you spent that time trying to create a new technology or new business or trying to improve the world, you would go far.

In order to prove cognitive dissonance, they put it to couples that wanted to have children, that having children only adds to the stress of life. That by having children you are adding to the stress of existence, not adding to the happiness. What did these couples say when faced with these facts? They said, that having children is the most beautiful thing in the world. Now why do they think like that? In my opinion it is because you get to them when they are young, when their minds are vulnerable to manipulation and you implant in them, this whole concept of the dream existence, where you are in love, married and a parent. You say to them, when you achieve this, you will be living the complete existence. It is brainwashing that makes everyone chase family, despite the fact that it leads to a more stressful existence. You brainwash the individual that this is how you become happy. Just like a religious fanatic, they are so brainwashed that they cannot even perceive that they are brainwashed. If you were mature you would not have children. If you were really mature you would derive your happiness from the simple fact that you are alive in this universe. It all rewinds back to what the economic system needs, and it needs children, just as flowers need sunlight. Thus, it markets the dream life of marriage and family as the means to claim the ever so coveted happiness. The economic system will never suggest living alone and being childless as the means to become happy, because that damages the system. It then implements this obsession with marriage and family, through the two threats. One, you will waste your life and two, you will be laughed at, should you not marry and have a family.

We attack religion, we attack criminality. We never think to attack economics or love

"I dream of a love that is more than two people craving to possess one another." - Irvin Yalom.

Insecure men and women suffer to love. This is why they remain unhappy because they hunger to have this person by their side.

True love is a social construct.

It is not enough to be a woman in this world; one must be a pretty woman. It is not enough to be a man; one must be a most wanted man. It is not enough to exist silhouetted against a dark indifferent universe; we must find someone to love before we can love ourselves.

Being in love does not necessarily translate into being happy.

Imagine for instance there is an intelligent life in another galaxy that must insert an electronic chip into the minds of their species in order to coerce them into reproducing. A horrible system, I think you would agree, for they are being taken advantage of. But what is the electronic chip equivalent in the human world of planet Earth? It is love. Love is figuratively injected into the minds of men and women and this then makes them seek out relationships, get married and have children. By doing those three things you are "living life to the fullest" or "making the most of existence." The reality is that the ulterior motive here is the economic system. It benefits from everyone trying to acquire "the dream life."

Marriage is forced upon men and women. They are under pressure to marry from parents, friends and co-workers. The fact that the individual's parents were married unconsciously enforces marriage upon the individual. Should the individual choose to deviate from this path of marriage, their parents will be disappointed in them. The same fear is evident in friendship or co-workers. That they are all in relationships again enforces the expectation on the individual who is not. All in all, the herd decides so much of our choices.

As alien as it sounds, the system uses romance to control society.

There is a willingness to fall in love which is a healthy quality to have, but there is also a desperation to fall in love which is a glaring sign of insecurity. I remember a woman remarking that she would rather marry twenty times and get divorced twenty times than never have married at all. This woman was immature. She was taught by society that she had to get married; no other option was viable.

One does not need all these commodities to be happy. You do not need love, friendship, money etc. All you really need is to exist.

A love shadowed by threats is no love at all. For example, a man must keep succeeding to be "loved" by his wife or a woman must keep being attractive to be "loved" by her husband. This is not love; this is an extortionate arrangement.

Are relationships nature or nurture? They are both. But sometimes nurture takes control. Through the Familiarity theory, the Framing effect, Normative Social Influence and also through the Labelling Anxiety, we get forced into being in one.

To hope to love one day is a terrific thing to have; but to be desperate to be loved is a disease. We talk about true love as if you must taste it. This is partly why there are so many insecure young men and women alive despite the luxury of the life they possess. They become brainwashed to believe that they must be in love to be happy. One must understand that love be it authentic or not is just a system, much like prostitution or solitude is. It is not something you have to do in life; it is something you can do. Anthony Storr: "It is only when we no longer compulsively need someone that we can love them."

You possess the incorrect attitude if you view the failure to be married as a failure.

Is it nature or is it nurture? Are we doing it because we instinctively gravitate towards it or are we doing it because we are told to?

The framing effect is so powerful. Relationships are framed by the environment, by culture and by society as this romantic, idyllic and a necessary phenomenon. "You have to be in a relationship, or else you will waste your life."

The whole world may adore you, but if you do not have a basic love for yourself, it will be redundant.

Take the two threats that I emphasize in my notes: the pursuit of happiness and the avoidance of stigma. Let's say you get invited to a wedding and you go alone. Firstly, apply the pursuit of happiness. So, you see all these other people with their partners at the wedding. What do you say when you observe these people? You say: "They look so happy." You say: "I cannot be happy until I have what they have." Which is love. Then the avoidance of stigma attacks your conscience. You think that by being alone without a partner, other people at the wedding are gossiping about you. You thus resolve to find a partner as soon as possible, just so you can avoid the nefarious stigma. Thus, you can see how these two threats combine to dictate our fate in life.

"Mature love is loving, not being loved." - Irvin D Yalom

Love seduces us with its romanticism, but romanticism does not translate into the dream life. Often it can make your life more difficult, especially if there are children involved. There is uncertainty associated with relationships. It is like placing a bet on a horse or sports team; there is risk involved. But such is the brainwashing of society, they must be in one and furthermore they expect it to be this dream life that they get told about. It is 50/50. It can go for you, but also against you. From an existential perspective, solitude is the most secure form of existence. Ask yourself: Which is more secure? Being happy alone or being happy by being dependent on someone to love you? But men and especially women are suckered into being in a relationship. They are afraid of being laughed at should they not be in one and they are also afraid of not living life to the fullest if they miss out in love. Consequently, a good number of people spend the glory years of their lives in unhappiness.

Friedrich Nietzsche: "Sometimes people don't want to hear the truth because they don't want their illusions destroyed."

There is nothing better than finding someone who is mature, grateful, who sees the beauty in life and existence itself. That is Authentic Love.

However, there is nothing worse than finding someone who is narcissistic, obsessed with material gain, that needs to be seen in love, that must be married. That is a narcissistic relationship.

The myth of true love is both the male's and female's greatest impediment. If you were to go around to schools and analyse pupils, you might find one male/female individual who is thinking about setting up a business. Statistically however you will find that most of the pupils are trying to make themselves as attractive as possible so that they will be liked. The point I am trying to make (and it sounds shallow) is that in order to be a millionaire by the age of thirty you must change your priorities.

I do not believe in true love; I believe in Authentic Love. That is a love wherein the two people have most importantly, each other. Love that is built out of the fabric of money, looks, background, intelligence etc. is not love. What would happen if all those privileges disappeared? The so-called love would disappear also. Honest love is when the individuals may have everything or nothing, but most importantly they have each other.

Is it not most ironic that the one thing we expect to yield happiness, is often the same thing that causes most distress! I am talking about love. If you are young and leveraging it all like a poker player on being delightfully happy when you are forty and are in love, you are more than likely going to be disappointed. Life is uncertain as Alexander Dumas would testify to. The trick is to be accepting of who you are when young and then go from there.

The narcissist loves the idea of love.

"If we did not look to marriage as the principal source of happiness, fewer marriages would end in tears." - Anthony Storr.

We are all drug addicts. If it is not heroin or alcohol, it is love or money.

Society knows what they want but not why they want. So, men and women especially are told that it is a necessity for them to be sexual. But they never possess the curiosity to question why they should be sexual. And to defy this eagerness to appear sexual is one step on the path towards freedom. Of course, the paradox is that if society were to negate this desire, the world would break down to a degree. But I still stand by what I say. You cannot be free if you are implicitly conforming. The method by which society behaves is akin to the drilled soldiers in a military camp. They are told to march or stop in unison. They all wear the same clothes and behave the same way. Society thus has it drilled into them repeatedly to form a relationship, raise a family and work. And what happens to that brave soldier who refuses to heed to the general's commands? He gets court martialled. He gets punished. Likewise, the individual that refuses to conform gets shunned by the herd. As I have said numerous times, it is fear as much as love that makes one conform.

Such is the power of the majority, that the person who cannot love is labelled psychiatrically defunct.

"Love is a decision, it is a judgment, it is a promise. If love were only a feeling, there would be no basis for the promise to love each other forever. A feeling comes and it may go. How can I judge that it will stay forever, when my act does not involve judgment and decision?" - Erich Fromm.

Commoditized relationship: This is where the symbol of the relationship provides more happiness than the actual relationship itself. For example, a man says internally: "Look at me, I'm in a relationship with this beautiful woman, therefore I must be happy." The actual projection of the relationship to his peers produces a sense of jubilation within. One must ask themselves: Am I happy because I enjoy the relationship or am I happy because I am seen in a relationship. If it's solely the latter, it's a commoditized relationship.

You are not your name, your face or your personality. You are when you cut to the core of existence, trillions upon trillions of atoms intricately woven together that obey the laws of quantum theory, who then are contained on a planet because of the law of general relativity. But the matrix of life becomes about relationships and careers. It becomes about falling in love and being approved. It becomes about making money and honing friendships. Man, despite the luxury of being the most intelligent species in this universe is still animalistic in his instinct. This lack of awareness, wherein the true realities of the universe are overshadowed by love and work, is in my opinion basic narcissism, but a narcissism that is vital to the economic system.

The anticipation of love, that one can share their life with someone, else is a healthy position.

We program the mind of the individual in such a way that they obsess over "finding the one," "being in love," "experiencing love" etc. The reality is that love is not a feeling, a sensation or an experience; it is a profession, it is a job and it is something you must learn.

It should always be happiness, then love; not love and then happiness. If you are happy within yourself and in your own solitude you will find love.

There is the madness of the minority, but one must not forget that there is also the madness of the majority.

Instead of falling in love with another person, why not fall in love with your place in this universe. Let life entice you.

One of the reasons why love is attractive is because we gain justification for this system daily. Parents, doctors, magazines, famous people all tell us that it is correct to date and get married.

"The individual has always had to struggle to keep from being overwhelmed by the tribe. If you try it, you will be lonely often and sometimes frightened. But no price is too high to pay for the privilege of owning yourself." I must have quoted this by Kipling countless times. But of all his masterful quotes, this is the one I would take everywhere with me.

Become a rebel and by this, I mean listen to your heart. Do not marry the person that makes you look good or provides for you. Marry the person you like.

The solitary path is not always the wrong path.

Conformity is an easy life; it is also a tragic waste of life.

To paraphrase Lenin, love is the opium of the obscure.

You marry for wrong reasons if you marry for aesthetic reasons.

There are so many ways to define your life. Love is one but not the only one.

The want to be desired is a nicer way of saying you want to be someone else.

"It is wrong to bear children out of need, wrong to use a child to alleviate loneliness, wrong to provide purpose in life by reproducing another copy of oneself. It is wrong also to seek immortality by spewing one's germ into the future as though sperm contains your consciousness!" - Irvin Yalom.

I remember reading about a woman who said that if she was not married by the age of thirty, she was breaking up with her long-term boyfriend. This woman was narcissism personified. She had all these targets she had to meet in order to be happy. She was living an inauthentic existence. The same applies to men.

I should probably say it more often, but I am not suggesting one does not get married and so on. What I am suggesting is that to get the most out of the said marriage, one must possess the correct attitude and overcoming narcissism is indicative of that. You cannot love if you are narcissistic.

Look at the adolescents. You will rarely find one that wants to live in solitude. In contrast, the standard adolescent male or female has said that they want to be married by the age of forty. Why do they think like this? They do so because we brainwash them to think like this.

If you look at the profitability of American Football or even soccer in England, the fans of those retrospective sports pour a lot of their income into supporting their team, in spite of the fact that the team doesn't care one iota about them. It is a poor deal for the fan, but an exceptionally good deal for the professional sports player. Now you must analyse why so many fans accept such a terrible proposition? A huge reason is because you brainwash them (the fans) when young to follow a certain team and in the quest to avoid boredom they become fanatical about supporting such and such teams. True love is something similar. It is something that is figuratively funnelled into the mind of the young child, and as such when they grow up, they do their utmost to try and find it. They just behave as the environment has told them to behave. And they are immature because of it. Like the casual sports fan, they are so absorbed in it, they cannot see how ridiculous it is. It becomes second nature to him or her.

The robust strong-willed individual is the individual who does not see a relationship as the be all end all.

We automatically deduce that our parents love us, everyone has them, they are looking out for the best things in our lives. Yes, but they are putting you under pressure to behave a certain way. It is the same with friends and co-workers. The more you associate with the herd, the more you are forced to adopt the herds ideology.

Where there is pattern there is method and where there is method there is an abundance of madness.

Do you want to be a machine, or do you want to be a human?

The individual finds it so hard to overcome the constraints of conformity. They are: A) Brainwashed immensely to conform; B) Afraid of being laughed at should they choose to deviate from the path; C) Afraid of "missing out in life" should they not find love or not become a parent. For example, look at men regarding sex. They are afraid of being laughed at by being a virgin. They are also afraid of "not living life to the fullest," by not having sex.

The phenomenal deceit: Telling you that by doing this or that, you are "living."

If we could not speak, sexual attraction would still exist, but this concept of true love would not. However, we could still be compassionate to each other. The umbrella term of true love is something we have engineered because we can speak.

Two souls can find each other in the vast darkness. They can take care of each other, they can please each other. This is Authentic Love. But a lot of these marriages are just convenient relationships. A lot of these marriages are just a fashion. Capitalism has told us that in order to be respected by the tribe we have to be married and be a parent.

A toxic relationship is one where we love the person because other people do.

I am not saying also that the rich man and the attractive woman cannot be compassionate towards each other or cannot find Authentic Love. They can. But they must be so careful. You must analyse your partner and ask: Is the person marrying me because they truly love me or because I make them look good? You have a responsibility to do this. An obvious example of this is when the female of society attaches herself to a man in high demand. Now she may get along amicably with him, but there is also the component that she looks good when seen by her peers with such a man.

The prisoner is enslaved by steel bars, the free man by the opinion of others.

Authentic Love exists, but it is not as common as you think. You cannot just get married and declare you are in love. This is what capitalism has told you, that once you exchange vows, one can assume they are in love. You must interrogate your soul and ask: If the world was ending tomorrow would I be with this person?

Telling yourself you must be married by a certain age is not love. That is fear. That is heeding to a fashion.

Fall in love with the universe and you will fall in love with your life.

It takes a level of maturity to fall in love. The insecure individual hungers for it, but their impetuosity prevents them from ever tasting it.

We hear of forced marriages with regards poorer economies. A woman is told by her parents to marry a certain man. This same pressure exists in capitalism, but it is invisible and silent.

One of the things I would search for before entering a relationship is maturity.

Mature people do not see the necessity of love. They do not obsess over this one person. They could end their relationship tomorrow without hesitation if needs be. If you believe in "the one" you are immature and insecure.

Whether you are male or female, you must turn down the person who is hyping you up to be what you are not. You must turn down the person who is obsessed with you, that leverages their happiness on you loving them and them loving you.

The system is set up so that the system will benefit. You automatically think that acquiring the dream life will yield the ever so desired happiness, as if human happiness is a universal constant in the laws of nature. It is not. They tell you: "this is how you become happy" because it benefits the system. That is why they emphasize love or marriage as a necessity to one's happiness. But what does the collective drive to find love truly benefit? It benefits the very system that told you to find it.

You can forgive the teenage boys or girls; they are immature and naïve. But you cannot forgive the 35-year-old man or woman who exclaims that because nobody loves them, they cannot be happy.

The system says: "You know what is really good? Having sex is." Then the system goes further: "Do you know what is even better? Having sex when "in love."" Then the system suggests something else even better: "Do you know what is the best of all? Having children with the person you are in love with." The system is always suggesting to the young impressionable individual that the key to becoming happy is to have sex, get married and have children. Why does the system suggest this? It does so because this is what benefits the system itself.

To learn how to love you must first learn how to live.

What we call love is compassion, understanding, responsibility and a genuine interest in the life of another.

The secure individual is confident they can enjoy life regardless of whether they find love or not. The insecure narcissistic individual sees no other path other than love. The insecure individual is so distorted by his or her capitalist culture that they must marry indiscriminately in order to feel good about themselves. This is nothing more than the power of social control.

Imagine two people wandering the landscape in a post-apocalyptic world where law and order have broken down. They are starved, cold, tired and hunted. But they stick together. There is no money, laughter, sex or image criteria to be met. This is Authentic Love. These are two people who have nothing except each other. Their bond, their love, rebels against nature. Now one must transfer this mechanism into the world as we know it today. Despite our existence in a world of peace, money, commodities, success, glamour, this exact mentality is needed to be truly in love. It is easy to proclaim you are in love when you have it all. Would that romance remain intact if you lost everything? That is the fundamental question.

Intelligent life from another galaxy would be laughing at us humans. They would laugh at the sincerity in which we believe in true love.

A relationship much like a shark must keep moving forward to survive. Love is a journey, frequently a fragile one, that never ceases.

Authentic Love in a sense must struggle to survive in this world. It is when things are going bad that it will reveal itself.

Love as Erich Fromm asserted is something that must be worked on. The individual must strive to improve their relationship, but they also must strive to improve themselves. Those in love must grow, as must their bond. They must mutate and resurrect themselves continuously.

"Love isn't something natural. Rather it requires discipline, concentration, patience, faith, and the overcoming of narcissism. It isn't a feeling, it is a practice." - Erich Fromm.

Love is not some natural instinctive response. It is a skill you can learn. It is something you can be taught.

Authentic Love must be one of the most beautiful experiences of being human.

Unfortunately, a healthy relationship takes two mature individuals. A relationship where one or both are not mature, is not healthy and will suffer.

Love is a discipline. It requires dedication and perseverance. It takes a great deal of maturity to be able to love. The standard capitalistic insecure individual will never experience it unless they mature. Narcissism is the enemy of Authentic Love.

"On the day when it will be possible for woman to love not in her weakness but in her strength, not to escape herself but to find herself, not to abase herself but to assert herself--on that day love will become for her, as for man, a source of life and not of mortal danger." - Simone De Beauvoir.

True love is really love for yourself.

In one sentence I can relay the mind-set of the insecure individual: "When I am in love, I will be happy." That is it. That is why they are not in love and consequently not happy. The genius Erich Fromm built a career out of that simple proposition.

The insecure individual falls in love to be labelled in love; they marry to be labelled married; they have children to be labelled a parent.

You do not fall in love; you cultivate your love. You do not fall into each other; you grow into each other.

Authentic Love is just a more precision engineered friendship. In order for two people to engage in Authentic Love, they must distance themselves from the herd, which is very difficult.

It is naïve to think you must just grow the relationship. You must also grow yourself.

Authentic Love is when you support each other, not depend on each other.

As absurd as it sounds, one must distance themselves from this mythical true love in order to engage in Authentic Love.

Maturity is a very endearing trait to possess.

The picture on the wall of the family unit in almost every home, is what seduces nearly almost everyone. That is what dictates their call. Just as a renowned architect may look with great pride at a finished building or stadium he or she has designed, the modern-day man and woman look at that picture with such satisfaction, that it fills them to the brim. That picture is what owns them and has since they were in adolescence.

You do not have friends; you are friends. "Have," is ego; it is narcissism. It is like having a house or a car.

Desperation is a by-word for insecurity.

The pseudo-prostitution marriage is one where they each individually give something to each other in return for something off each other, ergo trade. This trade usually manifests itself in terms of financial, emotional, security, sexual or image. Authentic Love in contrast is where they both grow their individual bond together. There is still trade but it is secondary to the singular love that they must work to cultivate. In the pseudo-prostitution marriage, when the trade fractures, the relationship disintegrates. With Authentic Love, the hurdles only make the bond stronger.

Capitalist marriage: They both give each other marriage because they both need to be married.

The choice for the person is simple: They can be a fashion, or they can be an individual.

"Love is a serious mental illness."- Plato.

The dark ocean that toils above and below us lies unperturbed.

The hunt to find love, if healthy, should not lead to insecurity. As in, for example, one should not have plastic surgery, designed to make them more sexually attractive, just to encourage someone to love them. That is insecurity.

The narcissist uses money, sex, image, security to declare they are in love. They may never explicitly say it, but their love is extortionate, for without the various luxuries the relationship would cease to exist.

I remember a woman once said she felt stigma in not having a boyfriend and in being alone. This is indicative of the terrible pressure that society is under to be in a relationship.

It is a mistake to say that because you have all these qualities that you are in love. Authentic Love is actually one of the qualities you have. It is part of your bond or link. The diseased individual says that because they have sex, money, image, security etc. they are in love. The mature individual sees love as another one of these qualities they possess. They may have sex, money, image and security, but they also have Authentic Love the quality.

Love is a reagent in the chemical reaction; it is not the product. Traditional thinking sees love as the product and that money, image, sex, emotion etc. are the reagents that when combined manufacture the product of love. This is a narcissistic or an immature version of love. Authentic Love is actually part of the equation of which the result is a relationship or bond.

The adversary is not men or criminals or life; the adversary is economics.

It is shallow to see your wedding day as the culmination of your existence.

"I should have become an "I" before I became a "we"." - Irvin Yalom.

You will rarely find an adolescent that has determined that they want to live in solitude and not get married. Statistically most adolescents want to fall in love, and they hold such a conviction because they have been brainwashed from youth.

Parenthood and education do two things. A) They make us behave a certain way. B) They make us afraid to step out of line or go against the current. Think of marriage with respect to these two things. A) We are told we must adopt the system of marriage. We are told this by the herd when young. B) We are afraid then to not get married because we will be the one deviating from the herd.

It is those in love who can be happy with nothing who can be happy with everything.

Just as we use the law to judge the morals of someone; we use love to judge their character. The man who visits escorts is dirty; the woman who chooses to live in solitude is odd.

Love the feeling is artificial. It will dissipate with time.

The world is so insecure, and this insecurity is worth trillions. It should be a criminal offense to be insecure.

The dream should not be the sun-kissed shores of Miami or the pavements of Madison avenue. The dream should be space, and only then would we see who we are.

A large part of being existentially free is trying to unlearn what your mind has learned.

Discover the better part of yourself.

Ask yourself why you cannot dare contemplate a world without marriage? The answer is because you have been hardwired to see marriage as a necessity of human existence when it is not.

The real prize in life is not accolades or monetary. It is the curiosity of finding things out for yourself.

"You have no responsibility to live up to what other people think you ought to accomplish. I have no responsibility to be like they expect me to be. It's their mistake, not my failing." - Richard Feynman.

The system sustains itself partly by convincing the individual it is not a system. Call the structure totalitarianism and its vilified; call it life and its condoned.

Our parents were brainwashed by their parents. Then they brainwash us.

If only we had the courage to live independently, we would be so much happier.

You do not have to do anything in life except die. That is the reality of it. So, when you remark that you must fall in love and get married as if your life depended on it, that is your infantile narcissistic demon rearing its head.

Erich Fromm's book The Art of Loving, should be compulsory reading for all adolescents. Fromm says many things in this great book and one of those things is that if you are infatuated with getting married you possess the incorrect skillset to thrive in that marriage.

In third world countries, they call it forced marriage. The exact same pressure exists in western society, but it is the individual who puts pressure on themselves. Granted they are severely influenced by the herd, but it is their own thoughts that condemn them. They are blessed with choice though; in that they can choose to defy the herd. But the brainwashing of the tribe from youth is so great, that this choice is seldom chosen.

Robert Frost: "Accept no one's definition of your life, define yourself."

A young woman discovers her husband is cheating on her. This destroys her. She feels broken and betrayed. Now imagine she had never known the man in question. Imagine she had never married and was content living alone. She would not have put herself in a position to be victimized. She would not have been broken or betrayed because she would not have been in a position to be. Relationships are not the most secure form of happiness; solitude is. The probability of being disappointed increases sharply when you depend on another human to be happy, be it friendship or love or perhaps both.

Life is two-dimensional to the immature. It is love and work. There is no universe, no atoms, no kidneys and liver and no awareness of the enormous chance that led to that individual being alive in this world as we know it. So consumed they are by conformity that they take it all for granted. Becoming a husband or wife is second nature to them. This is the result of their Economic Narcissism. They are so brainwashed that they cannot see they are brainwashed.

I am not suggesting that one lives like a hermit as Schopenhauer suggested. What I am trying to convey to the reader, be they male or female, is that if you want to thrive in a relationship, your attitude must be correct. If you are desperate to be loved or married, that is insecurity and you need to overcome this.

We yearn to fall in love and then when the relationship is not going as smoothly as it should, we blame the other person in the relationship. The reality is that the individual themselves must take some of the blame for being so desperate to be in a relationship in the first place. To depend on another person for your happiness is to play with dice. In other words, one could possess a much more secure existence if they depended on no one for their happiness.

We should be teaching our children about the universe and the enormous chance of life. Instead we teach them to conform indiscriminately as if their lives depend on it. Overtly we teach them that they must work to be happy; covertly we teach them that they must be in a relationship to be happy. This is the Economic Narcissism we instil in them. This is precisely why they are unhappy.

The insecure is more afraid of the consequences of not getting married than they are of getting married.

You marry the person who does not want to get married. It sounds so counter intuitive. You marry the person who does not leverage their whole existence in this universe on love.

Imagine if someone decided to disavow the rules of the road and drive on the wrong side. What would we think of this person? We would think they were eccentric or strange. This exact same mechanism applies to relationships. The individual is so afraid to not be in a relationship because they are threatened with being labelled dysfunctional.

The Paradox of Hedonism

"Happiness cannot be pursued; it must ensue." - Viktor Frankl.

The paradox of hedonism is linked to the narcissistic conformist. Such an individual is blind and only sees happiness through relationships and careers. But because they only see happiness through these elements, they distance themselves from becoming happy within them.

Very often the individual hungers to be happy through conforming because they wish to be seen happy through such a method. In other words, they wish to be labelled "happy." This however is a catch-22 because in trying to be happy one cannot experience happiness. This is called the Paradox of Hedonism.

Their narcissism instructs them to be happy, but that only dilutes any happiness they can receive. Suffering to be happy through gratification is not happiness.

The more one yearns to live the less they do. The more one tries to enjoy life the less they do. The more they try to be happy through looking happy (being labelled happy) the less happy they become. To actually be happy they must defeat their narcissism.

"To live only for some future goal is shallow. It's the sides of the mountain that sustain life, not the top." – Robert M Pirsig.

The narcissists often say they are missing out in life through not doing this or that. "I'm not socializing therefore I'm missing out on life etc." "I'm not married or in a relationship, therefore I'm missing out in life." What they don't realize is that through saying this they further push themselves deeper into the hole.

Those who enjoy life only do so because they do not realize it. If one tries to consciously attain happiness, they meet failure. They will not be gratified. Enjoyment or success is involuntary. It stems from the unconscious. Expecting to become happy will not bring happiness just more misery.

But this narcissist is so polluted by the labels of happiness (marriage and work) that they fully expect to be happy by becoming married and working an esteemed job.

Furthermore, one should ask themselves why is my happiness contingent on being in a relationship and succeeding at work? Why is it that one measures their happiness in terms of careers and relationships? We are human, we are condemned to make our own lives and our own philosophy. Yet billions are conscripted to retrieve their happiness through relationships and careers. They hold such convictions because they have been brainwashed to.

If you must force yourself consciously to watch a film or read a book it means you don't enjoy that film or book. The same applies to happiness. You cannot force yourself to consciously be happy. You must immerse yourself unconsciously in life and through doing that you become happy. But the caveat is that it is not guaranteed. Conforming may make you happy, but it may not, and you may force yourself to say you are happy through such an arrangement. But are you actually happy or just pretending?

This links to Sartre's Bad Faith. People pretend to be happy through conforming. They feign happiness. This is the Pretence Happiness. They pretend because life has told them this is how you are supposed to be happy. The narcissist in particular is devoured by this Bad Faith.

The thing about Pretence Happiness is that it is to be expected because we are severely constrained by the economic system. We have to work and as such if you are not actually happy, the next best thing is to pretend that you are.

It is not your divine right to be happy. You are an animal that can speak that has found a place in this universe.

The system preys on your desperation to be happy. If the system told you that you were expected to be married and have two children by forty, you would reject it. You would rebel against the system. So, what does the system do? How does it make you conform in a way that is not perceived as authoritarian? It does so by suggesting how you become happy and because you are above all else so desperate to be happy in life, you just believe what the system says. So, what is "becoming happy?" It is being married and a parent by forty. When you do that, you are living the dream life, apparently.

The pursuit of happiness is connected to the avoidance of stigma (The Labelling Anxiety), because it is through pursuing "happiness" that we are not stigmatized (not negatively labelled.) Happiness, from a sociological perspective, is not a dream, but a form of regulation.

People of a capitalistic heritage unconsciously assume that they deserve unconditional happiness. They do so because they unconsciously calculate that because they are from a certain background that they have an entitlement to happiness. Thus, they consciously attest that they should be happy through relationships and careers. Entitlement is systemic of narcissism.

You can only be happy; you cannot become happy. This is the error I observe repeatedly. The immature individual wants to become happy. They want to become happy in the future and they mistakenly believe they can obtain this elusive happiness by conforming. Yet they reach their forties, they have done what the system told them to do and they are not happy, only anxious and miserable. This is the Paradox of Hedonism. You cannot become happy; you can only be happy.

Furthermore, they abhor solitude. Alas as Erich Fromm speculated, it is the individual who can live in solitude who has the correct skills to succeed in conforming.

A "shot to nothing" in snooker, is when you attempt a shot but leave the cue ball safe should you miss that said shot. Life should be a mirror of this concept. Seek gratification, but also be grateful, should you fail to be gratified.

They brainwash you about how great A) Finding this one person is, B) Having sex with this one person, C) Marrying this one person and D) Having children with this one person. When you do this, you are living the complete existence and will be above all else happy. It is all lies, designed to make you conform so that you will contribute to the system. You cannot become happy by trying to be happy today, tomorrow, next year or twenty years down the line. You will not become happy; you will however waste time searching for a happiness you will never experience. That is the paradox of happiness. How then do you become happy? Be grateful for your existence in this universe.

I am not saying don't be in a relationship. What I am trying to convey is that the starting point should always be maturity and one of the defining points of maturity is the ability to live alone.

Nobody has a right to happiness and demanding happiness to be happy is the true instigator of anxiety and low self-esteem.

People go out to be liked and that is why they are not liked.

It is amazing that football is profitable. What does the footballer get out of it? Some make millions and as such you can understand why they do it. But what does the football fan get out of it? His team wins and he feels good for a couple of hours. And because of this he is prepared to spend a huge chunk of his income on this football team. It is madness. That we depend on things to make us gratified is a flaw in our psychology. Now apply this to work and relationships. We depend on these things to make us gratified, which in turn gives birth to a temporary happiness. The solution is gratitude and one should just look at the stars on a clear night and be grateful for being alive.

One needs to be more laid back rather than desperate to succeed. This applies to a job interview or love. If you are desperate to do well in an interview, you won't do well. If you are desperate to fall in love, you won't fall in love. Generally, those who enjoy life are the ones who don't take it too seriously. This is the paradox of hedonism. When the mind consciously tries to accrue success, it generally meets failure. I see this in real life relationships. An insecure individual is desperate to fall in love. They absolutely tie their self-esteem and self-happiness to being in love or to being seen in love. Because of this toxic eagerness to be in love, they never taste love. They are too immature, narcissistic and desperate to do so. You fall in love when you are not looking for it.

People "want an experience." When they walk into a shop, they want an experience; when they have sex, they want an experience; when they watch a film, they want an experience. This is exactly why they suffer and are unhappy, because they expect to be entertained daily. Then when they are not gratified, they complain. Life has not met their sense of entitlement. They are completely blind to the universe.

The internet is proof of widespread narcissism. For some on twitter or Instagram or facebook or quora, worth is calibrated through "likes." The more "likes" they get, the happier they feel about themselves. It is also the reason why they will never be happy.

They implant into your minds, much like the film Inception, the idea of the dream life and by obtaining it, you will above all else be happy.

The Easterlin Paradox states that more money increases happiness, but only to a certain point. That being super rich does not equate to more happiness.

"It is difficult to find happiness within oneself, but it is impossible to find it anywhere else." – Arthur Schopenhauer

If you stop depending on things to make you happy, you can ironically become happy. If you don't depend on someone to like you, if you don't depend on success, if you don't depend on earning money, if you don't depend on your football team to win, if you don't depend on meeting friends and partying, if you don't depend on having sex, you can become happy. The trick is to be grateful and to apply gratitude to your existence.

Modern man is a slave to desire. He needs to have sex, succeed, earn money, look well, hone friendships and so on, in order to be happy. But he never truly becomes happy; he becomes gratified, but the high wears off. It is like if you were thirsty and you drank seawater to quench your thirst. Initially you feel relieved. But in the long term, you suffer. That is gratification, in that your never become happy, but you continuously suffer.

Why is everyone's idea of happiness the same? We are both taught and constrained by the economic system. As it turns out we have little choice when the naïve individual is of the belief they have unlimited choice.

The universe isn't in existence to give to man. If that man is truly smart, he recognises that he must give back to the universe.

Your willingness to live should be because you are able to.

You generally find what you are looking for in life when you are not looking for it.

Some people are extremely poor; all they have is money.

One must take what the great film director Alfred Hitchcock said and it applies to all facets of life, be they engineering, art and love: "Between conception and execution you lose about 50% of what you intended." So, this dream life, I can guarantee will not materialize as planned. Then the sufferer is deflated when their romance ends, or they are not at a stage of their career they wished they were.

Nobody is pointing a gun to your forehead, saying conform to be happy. So why then is the insecure individual obsessed with conforming in order to taste this mythical happiness? They do because society has taught them to be. Society has taught them to be insecure.

Napoleon alluded to ribbons. Well, the modern-day ribbons, are sports teams, film stars, partners, friends, politicians etc. Why do we follow these things? Why do we leverage our happiness on these things?

What the capitalistic environment conveys to the individual is that they must be loved to be happy. What Buddhism conveys is that one must love their existence first in order to be happy.

Man is a most tragic animal. He wants to be happy, feels entitled to it, yet immerses himself in uncertainty, expecting happiness.

The mistake society makes is that they believe love guarantees happiness. It does not. It is akin to the poker player relying on calculated chance to be victorious. Sometimes the cards don't go his way, no matter how skilled he is.

You are unhappy because you hunger to be gratified. You say when you have a partner, a specific job, a family, a house, a car etc. you will be happy. But this is happiness contingent on being gratified. This is a narcissistic happiness.

You cannot be happy by wanting to be happy or pretending to be happy.

"The pursuit of happiness, thwarts happiness." - Viktor Frankl.

There are two types of insecure happiness. One, I call Strategic Happiness, in that the individual neglects being happy in the present, in favour of this dream of being happy in the future. For example, a female might say, "once I am a wife and mother, then I will be happy." Thus, all her energy is spent trying to reach the peak of the mountain, at the expense of the journey up it. The second type of insecure happiness is what I call Commoditized Happiness and is linked to Strategic Happiness. Such a person who suffers this insecurity leverages their happiness on other people approving them. As in when they live this dream life and people are impressed by this so-called dream life they live, then they feel glad. For example, an insecure man might say, "look at me, I am rich, have a beautiful wife, children, good job, own a nice house and drive a fast car. I look happy, therefore I must be happy." It is a narcissistic happiness. When people admire the life of such an insecure individual, that said individual in turn feels happy because people admire him or her.

We are constrained by the economic system. The lie promoted by the economic system is that by accumulating X, Y and Z, you can become happy. But what does this narcissistic happiness actually benefit? It benefits the very economic system that told the lie.

When you say "you have to," you attract anxiety. When you say: "you can," you relax. "I can get married, but it is not a necessity. I can have children but can live without them. I can work this certain job, but I also can work in another job."

The life of the insecure hinges on future gratification. The football team must win; the partner must fulfil their obligations; the targets at work must be met; the bills must be paid. He or she lives for future rewards and despairs in the present due to uncertainty. The mature person in contrast lives in the present. He or she conveys gratitude despite the uncertainty that abounds them. They recognise just how lucky they are to be alive and this realization negates the economic worries that afflict them.

"The only Zen you can find on the tops of mountains is the Zen you bring up there." – Robert M Pirsig.

It is a mistake to wait for your life to be perfect before you enjoy life.

Man is the only animal for whom existence is not enough. He needs to live, he needs to be happy, he needs to succeed, he needs to make money, he needs to have sex and so on.

Pretence Happiness: We play the role of what we deem happiness to be. Just as Goffman said we are actors, we pretend to be happy through conforming. In this, happiness is determined to be in a relationship, working the esteemed career, starting a family, owning a nice house, going on two holidays a year. This is how the system tells us to become happy and because people are so impressionable, they play this role of happiness, just like an actor in a film. "We are what we pretend to be so we must be careful about what we pretend to be." - Kurt Vonnegut.

The simplest way to procure happiness is to be grateful. The tides may ebb between success and failure, but with gratitude you can always be thankful for one thing and that is that you are alive.

Apply gratitude to your gratification. For example, a man dependent on his football team to win, in order to be gratified, should always have gratitude to fall back on, in case his football team loses. "So my team lost, but I am lucky to be alive and football is not the most important thing in my life." That is applying gratitude to your hunt to be gratified.

Exchange your desires for appreciation and you will have more than you ever need.

The system tells you how to be happy and through that mechanism, it controls how you live. If it told us how to live, we would revolt. We would rebel. Instead it suggests how to become happy. It implants in the mind, the idea of the accumulation of X, Y and Z, that supposedly leads to happiness. That is one subtle difference between capitalism and authoritarian countries

We are so desperate to be happy and that is what capitalism takes advantage of. It gets to children when they are young, it instils a narcissism in them, it then exposes them to each other and that then dictates a lot of their behaviour. The amount of people who are so afraid that they will not be happy if they do not find love. That is the level of manipulation we are facing. The individual is then led to believe that because they have millions in the bank and a loving family, that they are mature. They are mature with respect to the economic system; but they are not mature with respect to who they are.

"There is only one inborn error, and that is the notion that we exist in order to be happy. So long as we persist in this inborn error, the world seems to us full of contradictions. For at every step, in great things and small, we are bound to experience that the world and life are certainly not arranged for the purpose of being content. That's why the faces of almost all elderly people are etched with such disappointment." – Arthur Schopenhauer.

There is a sort of irony that is amusing, in that people want to be happy, it is the number one goal and yet they associate themselves with things that drastically reduce the chances of being happy. What am I alluding to? I am alluding to family. I am telling you that having a family drastically reduces your chances of being happy. Yet so many are of the opinion that they simply have to get married and have children. It begs the question, why? In my opinion it is the two threats that I mention, that have a huge role to play. A) You brainwash the individual on the dream life. "The accumulation of X, Y and Z is the path to happiness and if you do not follow this said path, you will waste your life." B) You threaten the individual with a negative label. "If you don't get married and have children, you will be the odd one out and will be demeaned." This fear has a huge reason why people, especially if they are insecure, conform. These two threats are solidified by socialization. The very thing that is often seen as the cornerstone of human existence, can work against us because the herd is at all times saying to us, this is how you live the dream life and this is how you are approved.

Psychiatric Illness

"Those who were seen dancing were thought to be insane by those who could not hear the music." - Friedrich Nietzsche.

If one sees their illness as something that shouldn't be part of them, they will never be happy. A huge component of the illness is the stigma of the illness. In other words that one can be labelled mentally ill hurts them along with their actual illness.

Part of their recovery is overcoming their narcissism which tells them that being psychiatrically ill is an incorrect label. Thus, such a narcissistic individual dreams of the day when they are free of their malady, which only serves to keep them trapped in despair.

The way to beat your illness is to embrace it as part of you. Psychiatric illness can be viewed as a breakdown or a break-through.

Such is the entitlement of western society who is drip fed capitalism three times a day, they instinctively compute that they deserve unconditional happiness. Usually this is in the mould of love and careers. When they struggle at these elements because of their psychiatric illness, they wallow in self-pity. "If only I didn't have anxiety; if only I wasn't ill." They use the label of their psychiatric illness to make themselves feel better. It reduces their cognitive dissonance.

Furthermore, they live inauthentic lives. They in ways adopt a false-self as Laing would put it. They cannot function through conformity (work and relationships) and yet they are resolute in adhering to this system. They convince themselves despite their malady that they must thrive in relationships and careers, even though their illness severely impacts their ability to do so.

"Life can only be understood backwards, but it must be lived forwards."- Soren Kierkegaard.

The reality is they are trying to procure the labels that designate happiness.

They try to justify their failure to be laudable amongst their peers by saying they are mentally ill. They exclaim that mental illness holds them back. It does not. Their own diseased mentality is what holds them back. They are using the excuse of mental illness to make them feel better through self-pity. They are using the label of mental illness to reassure themselves. Again, this is the narcissism rearing its ugly head.

They then turn to the psychiatric discipline to procure the elusive happiness. "Make me happy," they ask in a narcissistic tone. Only you can make yourself happy. You either work for this conformist happiness or you alter your thoughts and become happy through gratitude. Ask yourself: "Do I want to spend my whole life unhappy through self-pity or do I want to enjoy my time in this universe?"

Furthermore, we automatically deduce that people who do not conform must be mentally ill. The homeless man who refuses to live as normal folk do is suffering some psychiatric malady. But imagine for instance a world of anarchy where law and order has broken down. In that world the mentally ill would be considered normal. Thus, it can be assumed that mental illness is a derivative of an economic functioning world.

"The fact that millions of people share the same form of mental pathology does not make these people sane." - Erich Fromm.

Instead of treating the individual suffering from depression/anxiety we should treat the cause of their psychiatric illness, which is ultimately the economic system.

Their anxiety or illness is a direct response to life itself and not independent of it. When they immerse themselves in the world, they feel anxious.

What they fail to realize is that their illness is not independent of life but rather it is part of the fabric of who they are and as long as they keep wishing to be cured, they will never be cured. To beat your illness, you must accept it as part of you and go from there. If you keep looking in the rear-view mirror you will never see forward.

When the insecure psychiatrically ill individual triumphs over their inherent narcissism, they can live with their illness. Thus, they become grateful.

"Society is an insane asylum run by the inmates." - Erving Goffman.

Is it that the mentally ill are different or are that the healthy minds are too numerous?

Madness is subjective.

Stand in the centre of a busy shopping centre, look around you and you will see the madness.

Anything that is dysfunctional to the economic system is labelled negatively. Psychiatric illness meets this criteria. But what if psychiatric illness is not illness per se. What if it is just an alternative response to life (the economic system) as we know it?

The herd then in their impetuous naivety believe what the powers that be tell them about psychiatric illness. It is perceived as something foreign, toxic and something you should not have. In other words, it becomes negatively labelled by society.

To believe in a god is religion; to believe you are god is insanity.

One's anxiety is being caused by their response to the world (specifically the economic system) and yet they continue to engross themselves within the world expecting a different result each time. A common complaint is: "I'll get there some day." This is the inauthenticity of their existence. They are failing in a system they continue to believe they will succeed in. You will get there if you embrace your illness as part of you. It will end when you stop trying to live this life you feel you are supposed to live. The dream life is a system and as a system it does not benefit everyone. But you can find a system you can be rewarded from.

Does your mental illness cause your poor response to life or does your poor response to life cause your mental illness? The naïve person thinks their failure in life is because of their mental illness. What they fail to recognise is that their response to life is what causes their mental illness. In other word's their response to the environment (relationships; work; friendship; the economic system etc.) is defective and the product of this is their mental illness. It is not mental illness that inhibits them; it is that they can't function in this conformist life. But they can find another model in which they can function. To give you an example of what I mean: A person who is schizophrenic may state that their psychiatric illness inhibits them and so on and therefore they struggle. The actual reality is that life (the environment) causes their illness. Their schizophrenia is a direct result of interacting with the world. It is the individual's unique response to life.

You do not want the day you die to be the first day you become free of anxiety. You are going to have to accept that you cannot live this popular life of relationships and careers. But you can find a life you can live.

Who is ill? Those who cannot live with people or those who cannot live without them?

I see it so much. They yearn to be sociable but being sociable causes anxiety. They yearn to be in a relationship but being in a relationship causes anxiety. They yearn to be working this esteemed career but such a career causes anxiety. Yet they keep trying or probing this existence and as they keep doing this, they keep becoming anxious. They have been brainwashed by conformity to only see happiness in terms of conforming, but the irony is they cannot succeed in this system.

By far the most common complaint with regards mental health is low self-esteem. The sufferer is either not smart enough, not attractive enough or not sociable enough or perhaps all three and these are all simply different ways of saying they are not liked enough. What they are in fact doing wrong is measuring their self-esteem in being wanted and thus when they are not desired their self-esteem takes a battering, enhanced by self-pity. The solution is not to better themselves in these areas, as they would instinctively conclude. No, the solution to their problems is to not measure their self-esteem in being coveted. In other words, to be grateful for just being alive in the first place.

"Be like a rocky promontory against which the restless surf continually pounds; it stands fast while the churning sea is lulled to sleep at its feet. I hear you say, "How unlucky that this should happen to me!" Not at all! Say instead, "How lucky that I am not broken by what has happened and am not afraid of what is about to happen. The same blow might have struck anyone, but not many would have absorbed it without capitulation or complaint." - Marcus Aurelius.

That the person we label normal does not see other people as threats is an illness in itself. But because this illness benefits the economic system, it is extoled.

Despite all the depression and even suicide caused by the economic system, we never change the economic system.

Think about it: A psychiatrist and a person suffering delusions are stranded on an empty island. Who is sane and who is insane in such an arrangement?

Why don't we lock up all those who follow a sports team? Isn't that madness. Why don't we lock up all those who believe in this mythical love?

Isn't that madness. Why don't we lock up all those who believe in some fairy in the sky? Isn't that madness. You see if the madness benefits the majority and hence benefits an economy, that madness is normalized.

Is one mad or is reality just insane?

Do not kill yourself; it would be just another indifferent event in a gloriously indifferent universe.

You must do two things. A) Discover your limitations and B) Accept them.

Reality is the madness. Isn't the coincidence beautiful. All the behaviour that psychiatry labels illness, is the same behaviour that is detrimental to the economic system. Just exquisite.

Once you stop perceiving your mental illness as something that impedes you and start seeing it as something that is part of you, you stand a better chance of becoming happy.

You can be your own psychologist and you do not need to study anyone else. You just need to study yourself.

A good psychologist studies people; a great psychologist studies himself.

Is psychiatric illness an illness or is it something that does not afflict the majority? What I am trying to convey is that what we establish as healthy behaviour, what we deem criminal behaviour and what we determine to be psychiatric illness is not a constant of nature. We have as an intelligent species determined that such and such behaviour is correct and other behaviour is incorrect.

One of the most common things I hear or read is that the sufferer says: "It will get better." I remember reading about a guy who said he was suffering from anxiety and depression because he did not have a girlfriend and did not have a good job. Then when he got a good job, he managed to get a girlfriend and suddenly he was cured of his depression and anxiety. In his own words, he attested that his life "was now good." Now analyse why his mood improved. It was not because he cured his depression but rather it was because he managed to meet the requirements of conformity (a good job and a relationship). Thus, when he met these targets, he felt good about himself and his depression vanished. When he was labelled appropriately, he felt good. This was the result of his inbred narcissism that convinced him that he could only be happy through meeting certain stipulations. Now this is what I have said in my notes and previous notes. People measure success not on the fact that they are alive in this universe. No, they measure it in terms of hitting targets, ergo, relationships and careers. They measure it in terms of being labelled correctly. Now this is a precarious position to hold for the man in question, for what happens if the crutch is kicked from under him. If his relationship broke up or he lost his job, his depression and anxiety would return. So, what can one do? They can try and measure success differently. Instead of taking the capitalistic method of being happy (relationships and work), you adopt a Buddhist or existential or Stoic mechanism. This is where you display gratitude because you realize you are so lucky to be alive. This is where you do not care about relationships or working the pretty job. This is where you realize that being alive is the greatest achievement of your existence. Thus, when you think like that you rid yourself of your Capitalistic Insecurity and discover a concrete and lifelong happiness. Your life "can get better," if you just change the way you think. It is that simple.

The insecure are all the time comparing themselves to other people. This is Social Comparison Theory. They see themselves as failures when they contrast themselves to someone who is rich or beautiful. They then remark that if only they had what that other person had, then they would be happy. Would they? It is a rhetorical question because I do not think that even if their dreams came true, they would be happy. The reason being is that they are insecure or narcissistic. Their whole methodology of thought is diseased. They do not need to become rich or beautiful to be happy; they need to change their mentality.

We know what we desire but seldom do we know that we are often incapable of obtaining what we desire.

Life is not miserable; it is your response to life that makes it miserable.

"My fear is my substance," said Franz Kafka, "and probably the best part of me." You must turn your weaknesses into your willingness to live. Kafka is arguably the greatest writer of the 20th century because he did just that. Instead of bemoaning the fact that you have psychiatric problems, use those maladies to your advantage. Use your weaknesses as your strength; use your insecurities to build a brighter future.

Delusion is hearing voices. It could easily be supporting your local team or being obsessed with how you look.

You are not a victim; you are a survivor.

There is the madness of the minority, which is obvious: Schizophrenia, bipolar, OCD etc. But there is also the madness of the majority and it is called conformity.

"Society highly values its normal men," said Laing. Yet these normal men are responsible for most of the tears shed on this planet.

The psychiatric question should not be what is wrong with you. It should be why are you different.

The sufferer refers to themselves as broken but as Hemingway said: "The world breaks everyone and afterwards many are strong at the broken places." I suppose we are all broken in some ways, even the individual who has it all. The happiest people find solace in this shattered existence.

Then the paradox of hedonism kicks in. The sufferer remarks that they wish to feel happy and in doing so condemns themselves for one cannot consciously claim happiness. One can only immerse themselves in life and hope that the result is happiness or gratification. But the problem as alluded to is that this system, this capitalistic mechanism cannot provide happiness for the sufferer, only an unbearable anxiety and sometimes depression. Thus, the cycle repeats itself. The sufferer puts themselves into the world, they then feel anxiety and retreat, they then wallow in defeatism and remark that they wish they could be happy through conforming and they then go back out into the world to try and feel happiness, but are met only with despair. A cycle of Attack/Withdrawal thus prevails.

The system of Attack/Withdrawal is the mechanism by which the sufferer oscillates between immersing themselves in life, then retreats from life because it is too stressful and then after a period of time immerses themselves in life again hoping for a different outcome (chiefly reward or happiness). But the overriding emotion felt is one of anxiety.

I do not doubt that the behaviour of schizophrenia or bipolar is different. But is it an illness or is it just something that is dysfunctional to the current economic system?

I remember quite vividly reading about a woman who attested she had lost ten years of her life to mental illness. The tragedy was that as long as she held such a tainted conviction, she would lose the next ten as well. It was not mental illness that was haunting her; it was her perception that it was mental illness to blame for her poor quality of life. This was systematic of her narcissism which told her that she could not be Borderline PD and instead had to be married and working to be of esteem. In order for this woman to mature and to become happy she had to overcome her narcissism.

If you can see the universe, you will see more, you will see truth.

Madness is doing what everyone else is doing and not seeing the madness in it.

Just because they are the herd, does not mean they are not brainwashed.

The surest way to remain unhappy is to continuously see yourself as a victim. You are not a sufferer of psychiatric illness; you are a survivor of psychiatric illness.

It is so easy and so rewarding to blame mental illness for your perceived failure.

A man once said: "I just want what everyone else has." This is self-pity.

Human Beings are the only animal that needs to be liked in order to be happy.

To know what you can do you must first determine what you cannot do.

So many problems stem from the fact that we want to live in a perfect universe.

Psychiatry has a habit of placating the conforming class.

We have become so desensitized to normality that we cannot see its madness.

A by-product of the current economic system is psychiatric illness. We remark it's a product of being human but it's also a product of the economic system imposed on us.

The world is the asylum and we just cannot see it.

"The only place where success comes before work is the dictionary," said the great American Football coach Vince Lombardi. In order for you to reprogram your mind to convey gratitude will take work. Although these notes may inspire, it will take perspiration to rewire your mind.

Do not hate your psychiatric illness because it will then hate you. Love it. Consider it part of your response to life. You beat it by fighting with it rather than against it. It can be breakdown or break-through.

There are some people who should not be in a relationship or have a family or even work. They lack the skills and resources to succeed in these things. Yet they are resolute in doing these things. If a doctor or person of note suggested not to get married or become a parent, they would retort that they were entitled to do so.

We should get counselling because we go to see counsellors.

The fear of not living is often worse than actual living, especially for the insecure. They are sedated by the guilt of not living "the good life."

The eagerness to interact with another human being is a psychiatric illness.

Madness and normality are frames of reference. Neither one is more correct than the other, only more convenient.

If you took someone who was psychotic and someone who was deemed normal and introduced them to intelligent life from another galaxy, that intelligent life would not be able to deduce who was normal and who was ill.

Self-pity

"Self-pity is the worst possible emotion anyone can have. And the most destructive." – Steven Fry.

Self-pity is so common amongst western society. It is a derivative of narcissism. It stems in part from the eagerness to be labelled correctly. Such individuals are not labelled correctly by society and as such blame life for not providing for them.

Those who grow up in wealth have unrealistic expectations for life. They expect because of their environment that they deserve the dream life and furthermore they expect to receive it effortlessly. When life fails to materialize in this narcissistic individual, they can only blame the environment for their failure.

This is a narcissistic self-defence: Blame something or someone else for one's failure. This narcissistic self-pity reassures them that they are not to blame for their woe. Again, one reduces their Cognitive Dissonance through self-pity.

Self-pity is the most toxic of emotions to possess. Self-pity will destroy you. It will prevent you from being happy.

Self-pity is a quite common complaint from one who is unhappy with who they are. It is a symptom of low self-esteem. To rid yourself of it, you must first do battle with narcissism.

People in their quest to be happy basically turn to doctors and say make me happy.

One must understand that it is easier to treat the positive symptoms of schizophrenia than it is to treat someone who has chronic low self-esteem.

People say they did not have a good childhood and they use this as an excuse to wallow in defeatism. If you keep yearning to have had a good childhood, you will never become happy. Do not let the past dictate who you are. You are alive and healthy now.

There is an endemic of low self-esteem fuelled by self-pity. A common complaint in this capitalistic environment is that the individual is unattractive or unpopular amongst his or her peers. This is not psychotic depression. This is low self-esteem. This is attesting that because the herd does not label you appropriately, thus you cannot be happy. It is narcissism.

Self-pity is a product of the capitalistic environment that makes one insecure. It is a direct consequence of the Capitalistic Insecurity. Such individuals are conditioned on relationships, love, popularity, image, careers to be gratified and hence happy. Thus, the first words in the mind of the individual who pities themselves is "if only." "If only I was in a relationship, I would be happy; if only I had that job, I would be happy; if only I looked more attractive, I would be happy." They are all the time yearning for more in life and the reality of their existence in this barren universe is taken for granted. And the outstanding irony is that even if all their dreams came true and they lived this dream life, they would still wallow in self-pity, because they are diseased individuals and this psychiatric disease is called narcissism. What they need to be happy is not the realization of their dreams, but a counsellor that would try to pull them out of this toxic mentality they possess.

It is a contradiction that people are blind to. They want to be happy, but their lifestyle that they want to make them happy is drenched in uncertainty. For example, relationships, we want to be happy by being in one, yet by being in one we increase the uncertainty and hence decrease the chance of being happy. It is chance to depend on someone else to be happy. Yet society is resolute. They must be in one; there is no other choice. So, they spend most of their youth unhappy all because they want to be happy in something that does not guarantee happiness. You then suggest that they do not need the relationship or the esteemed career or the family nucleus and they will dismiss you.

If you are continuously waiting for medication and psychologists to make you happy, you will never be happy. Part of becoming happy is taking control of your own life and determining your own thoughts.

Irvin Yalom once said that the key to being happy is realizing you cannot change what happened in the past.

A patient once said: "I want to go back in time and not mess everything up. I want to go into the future and everything to be great." This person will never be happy.

Existence is the ultimate free lunch. You should not be alive.

The physicality of death destroys us, but the idea of death saves us, in that it can make us appreciate life more.

Doctors cannot beat self-pity. They cannot live your life for you. What they can do is tell you that you are absorbed in self-defeatism.

No one can make you happy except yourself. The best psychologist in your life is yourself. It is your own perspective that determines who you are.

Cognitive Dissonance: I remember reading about a man who wanted a scientific reason for why he was not "good with the women." To reduce his cognitive dissonance, he latched onto this whole Love Shyness clique. It is the same with self-pity. We want reasons for why we have failed, in order to reduce our dissonance. "It is life's fault; if only that had not happened; if only I had this." Self-pity is a method of reducing your cognitive dissonance.

Nihilism, as counter intuitive as it sounds, can be therapeutic. Your relationship may end, your parent may die, you may lose your job, you may struggle to pay bills and feed your children, but you can always comfort yourself by the fact that you are alive in a universe that does not want you to be alive. When you are plagued by the anxieties of life, you can comfort yourself by the fact that you will not find another human being in all the galaxies in the observable universe.

Celebrities make people insecure. They (the celebrities) post pictures about how happy they are on their holiday and the insecure individual gets it into their head they need the same to be happy. The individual is always comparing themselves to other people. "If only I had what they had." This is Social Comparison Theory and the Labelling Anxiety. One, in order to mature, must stop comparing themselves to others and must overcome their fear of being negatively labelled.

You and you alone are held accountable for how you perceive life. It is your own thoughts that determine who you are.

The tragedy of life is that we know everything about the world, but nothing about ourselves. We know what we want but not why we want what we want.

"Forces beyond your control can take away everything you possess except one thing, your freedom to choose how you will respond to the situation.

You cannot control what happens to you in life, but you can always control what you will feel and do about what happens to you." - Viktor E. Frankl.

The travesty of those under the capitalist shadow is that they are often economically secure but emotionally insecure.

How many men and women possess low self-esteem over their failure to be deemed attractive by the herd?

A drug improves your mood, but it cannot alter peoples attitude towards you and more importantly it cannot alter your response to their attitude towards you.

The western man does not worry about food; he eats three meals a day. He does not worry about shelter; he lives in a mansion. He does not worry about money; he has multiple bank accounts. So, what does he worry about? He worries simply about whether he is liked.

Self-pity is a product of education. You instinctively learn that when the herd appreciates you, you feel content. Thus, the individual who is not appreciated feels disconsolate and finds substance in self-pity. Ultimately, they forget how fortunate they are to be alive in this universe.

To the insecure, they believe that all life's problems can be solved by being another person.

Of course, there are people who suffer from severe depression or bipolar or another severe mental illness. But there are many whose complaint is feeling depressed when the source of their problem is low self-esteem mainly due to not living this fantasy life.

Man is the only animal who is aware of the universe and yet he turns a blind eye to it. You would think it would set him free or that it would make him appreciate how good it is to be alive. However, he still cannot free himself of his animal instincts. It's just these animal instincts are love and careers.

We do not need another world. We need more mirrors.

You are your own teacher, your own psychologist, your own god.

"When you arise in the morning, think of what a precious privilege it is to be alive - to breathe, to think, to enjoy, to love." - Marcus Aurelius.

One can learn so much from the stoics. Stoicism teaches one to mature and appreciate the universe. It teaches one to overcome gratification and instead be grateful. Happiness lays not in what you have or in living the dream life but rather in how you think.

Just like the alcoholics and the drug addicts all associate with each other, the sufferers of self-pity all immerse themselves in each other. By doing this they gain sympathy and validation among other things. "Oh, I had an argument with someone close to me today; well it wasn't your fault." "Oh, I'm never going to live this normal dream life; well it's the illness, it's not you." All this does is increase the reptilian self-absorption. All it does is sink the sufferer further into the pit of self-pity.

"You either get bitter or you get better. It's that simple. You either take what has been dealt to you and allow it to make you a better person, or you allow it to tear you down. The choice does not belong to fate, it belongs to you." - Josh Shipp.

Men and women are always probing themselves unconsciously. Capitalism has in a sense drugged them. "I need," is probably the most common thing they say to themselves and its often unconscious and instinctive. "I need a relationship; I need a good job; I need to be happy." They do not even realize they are saying it. But their habitual life is dominated by this dream existence they must live. They may never say these things overtly, but their mind is drenched with this conformist propaganda. It keeps attacking them internally such is their capitalist brainwashing. It is like Iago, feeding them lies about how to succeed or be content. They automatically attest that they must live a certain life in order to enjoy it. From adolescence this mind-set haunts them. It shadows their day to day activities. "I need to find love; I need to make money; I need to be endorsed." It poisons their thoughts. Their mind is programmed in such a method that it keeps harassing them with "I need." Ultimately because they keep saying unconsciously in various ways "I need," they never actually become happy. They never discover any semblance of happiness in this universe. They then grow old and lament the time they wasted being in anxiety over their failure to meet the stipulations of conformity.

Women, those that are insecure, instinctively attest that they need to be attractive; they leverage their self-esteem on it. Men, those that are insecure, instinctively attest that they need to be successful; they leverage their self-esteem on it. Now there are many more permutations of "I need." Analyse yourself. Count how many times you say to yourself without realizing it: "I need," or a variation of it. This is the disease of gratification. When we get what we need, we feel good. But what if we lose them or never get them?

Instead of saying "I need," say "I have."

Traditional thought: I am not happy because the person I like does not like me. Existential thought: I am lucky to be alive in this universe, therefore I do not need this person to like me in order to be happy.

Recovery is to not feel depressed. Another part of your recovery is to boost your self-esteem and to refuse to wallow in self-pity.

We all dream of a better future, but sometimes you must give up the hope of a better past.

In the capitalist culture we are so used to buying or obtaining our happiness. We buy a new car and feel good. We buy a new set of clothes and feel good. We start a relationship and feel good. We advance in our career and feel good. We are thus agents of gratification. These things make us happy; they make us gratified. People thus develop a mentality where life is expected to comfort them or make them content. It is as if they were put on this planet to unconditionally receive pleasure. Now the mentally ill person in western culture possesses this mentality. They start from the offset that life should provide for them unconditionally. They concoct this dream life where they are married and working. When events fail to materialise, they become distraught. Furthermore, because they are so infected with this capitalist gratification they turn to psychiatry and psychologists to make them "happy." When that avenue fails, they blame the psychiatrists and psychologists for failing to make them happy. Little do they realize that they must work themselves to become content. But they are so used to having everything in this capitalist culture that they do not want to work.

"Life is not always a matter of holding good cards, but sometimes, playing a poor hand well." – Jack London.

In order to be happy, one must display an attitude of gratitude. If you do not wake up each day in love with your existence, you are doing it wrong.

Life does not make you happy; your response to life is what makes you happy.

There is no magic pill that can suddenly make you happy. You either must work for it or you change the way you think.

It is better to have suffered to taste life than to never have tasted it at all.

Whenever I feel sorry for myself, I think of Helen Keller. She was blind and deaf and yet an incredibly happy person.

Self-pity is when you see yourself as a victim of a crime in which life was the perpetrator.

You can be a victim in life, or you can be a survivor and there is a difference.

Gratitude is a most potent venom.

You are not what has been done to you; you are what you do with what has been done to you.

You can dream of this landscape where you are saved, or you can make this dream a reality through saving others.

Trying to be yourself is normal behaviour; trying to be liked is low self-esteem.

A common inference when sabotaged by self-pity is the yearning to feel normal. But the more one tries to be normal, the more difficult it becomes.

People do not want to acknowledge they are not good enough; they want a reason for why they are not good enough. Self-pity provides that reason. "If only this had not happened; if only I had this."

The self-pity of the middle to upper class citizens of western society and perhaps other societies is just toxic to view. They have so much, so much more than the starving and suffering people of Africa and other areas and yet they continue to wallow in pity because of some small miniscule matters. The big issue is that they are not living this dream life where they are popular, sociable, rich, good looking, devoid of mental illness etc. and because they don't have these things, they ignore the luxury they do have. Self-pity amongst the people of the first-world countries is one of the most sickening habits of humankind. I can forgive the refugee or the homeless man for complaining about a lack of food or a lack of a comfortable living standard. I cannot forgive the individual who complains about a poor quality of life because they are not popular or good looking enough. Self-pity is the most nauseating, the most repugnant, the most cancerous of all the personality traits you can possess.

Be in absolute love with this universe and your place in it.

I always think of Lou Gehrig's mentality when he was diagnosed young with Motor Neuron Disease. You would automatically think he would be bitter, given that he was in the prime of his career when the disease hit him. "Damn life; it's all life's fault," you would think he would say. Instead he came out and said he was the luckiest man to exist given the life he had lived, even though he only had less than two years to live. People should mimic Lou Gehrig. Be grateful despite your problems. Isn't a life with problems still much better than no life at all. If you want to learn how to live, read Lou Gehrig's speech.

I remember reading Richard Dawkins The Selfish Gene and he remarked that half an eye is still better in evolutionary terms than no eye at all. Similarly, with existence from an existential perspective, a life with problems is still better than no life at all.

The self-help market, which is worth billions annually, is an embarrassment for humanity. If alien life were to observe us, they would be stunned at how unhappy we are despite our dominance and intelligence. There are two obvious problems: A) We are desperate to be "happy," and B) We believe we can become "happy" by buying these books.

"Sometimes the world we have is not the world we want. But we have our hearts and imaginations to make the best of it." - Elizabeth Bishop.

Do not buy another self-help book; write your own instead. Do not pay another person to study you; study yourself instead.

The rescued abused animal does not do two things: Wallow in pity and seek vengeance.

You cannot determine what happened to you, but you can determine how you respond to what happened to you.

I once read that the toughest journey a human takes, lays in the seconds they are born. Thinking like that makes all your obstacles in life surmountable. Life and its struggles are a gift. Find meaning in the suffering as Frankl noted.

"The heart of man is very much like the sea, it has its storms, it has its tides and in its depths it has its pearls too." - Vincent van Gogh.

Chapter Three
Existential Maturity

"You have everything needed for the extravagant journey that is your life."
- Carlos Castaneda.

The opposite to the Labelling Anxiety (in part) is existential maturity/freedom. For one to fully grasp existential maturity they must first overcome their inbred narcissism. They must overcome their fear of being labelled negatively.

The existentialists remark about authenticity. I would go further. One must become authentic to the universe. They must become aware of the nihilistic realities of the world they inhabit. Through doing this they gain maturity in that they overcome their narcissistic brainwashing. They must overcome their Economic Narcissism.

The narcissists only see love and work. They are blind to the universe. Existential maturity involves turning away from love and work, towards the universe.

What Existential Nihilistic Therapy sets out to do is make one grateful.

What Existential Nihilistic Therapy sets out to do is make you aware of the universe because when you do that life becomes absurd and with this absurdness accompanies appreciation. We really take life for granted. It becomes about work, relationships, money, family, sports etc. But such a life as I have remarked in the notes is laced with anxiety and suffering. So henceforth I endeavour to make you see the absurdness of existence and in doing so you come to recognise how lucky you are to be alive.

What Existential Nihilistic Therapy sets out to do is make people triumph over their narcissistic Labelling Anxiety. One must overcome their fear of being laughed at. To do this one must triumph over narcissism.

To become happy through existential nihilism one must battle with the power of the unconscious. Since childhood, your mind has been infused with propaganda pertaining towards capitalistic gratification. Thus, to alter your mentality you must retrain your unconscious. You must unlearn what you have learned. This is not easy. It takes years of self-psychoanalysis. But gradually you begin to reach the promised land of happiness. Gradually you begin to convey gratitude for just being alive.

I cannot emphasize it enough: You need to know less people to be more secure. Every person you expose your identity to is another person who labels you. Think of the anxiety of the criminal when caught. He is exposed to the world through news media. Or think of the famous person. You must apply that same apprehension to the law-abiding individual. Once you become known you become labelled and this labelling makes you insecure. Once known you are imprisoned by the interpretation of the person or persons who know you. Think of the Labelling Bind. Your boss or your partner asks you to do something, that you do not wish to do. But in order to maintain a positive label, you wilt and do that something. This is the threat that people pose.

One must self-analyse and ask: Why do I cling to this idea of love and work to be happy? Why can't I be happy just to exist? Stare into a mirror and ask yourself do you want to feel happy? If the answer is yes, then you must change how you think.

When you watch a good film, you feel glowing after it is finished. This state of euphoria lasts for about an hour, but then wanes and finally disappears and then you must watch another film to get high. Thus, when you read notes about existentialism that inspire you, the feeling is only temporary. Then you forget the dichotomy and must like an addict experience another high. Thus, the power of the notes is nothing unless you are prepared to work and challenge your unconscious. No one can do it for you. No one can learn it for you. You as an individual are tasked with that.

The opposite to this gratification is an attitude of gratitude. This is where you display appreciation every day or every second for which you exist. This is a happiness that cannot be taken from you.

If the world were ending next week, the common laws would break down and anarchy would reign. What I am trying to convey is the laws of society as we know it are not set in stone. Rather we adopt them to placate the system of economies. Men and women then become consumed by this methodology of life.

Existential Nihilistic Therapy in one sentence: Human existence is absolutely worthless; enjoy it while you can.

It is not that we forget, but rather that we do not realize that we are alive not in this town or country or even planet but in this universe. We do not realize how lucky we are to be alive. We do not realize the enormous chance that spawned intelligent life in this planet. The disease of capitalism that was ignited through education poisons us. Happiness becomes relationships and work. That we are so lucky to exist escapes us.

Look at adolescents. They are not obsessed with the perplexity of the atom or the wonder of the universe. More than likely they are obsessed with relationships and work and that is a huge reason why they are insecure.

Recognise just how fortunate you are to be alive in this universe. Do not think of your town or your country. Think of this universe and your fortunate standing in it.

We are teaching adolescents the wrong way. We inadvertently teach them that the only way you can be happy is by being married. Thus, their whole life is built towards being married on the assumption that they will become happy. Then they get married and are drenched in uncertainty and chaos because they must continue to work to maintain the marriage and hence happiness. We should teach them to be grateful. We should teach them to see life as a gift. Then they will possess the skillset to become happy.

"It has been said that astronomy is a humbling and character-building experience. There is perhaps no better demonstration of the folly of human conceits than this distant image of our tiny world. To me, it underscores our responsibility to deal more kindly with one another, and to preserve and cherish the pale blue dot, the only home we've ever known." - Carl Sagan, Pale Blue Dot.

In your darkest hour, when all hope has faded, try to think of the universe and how insignificant you and your troubles are in it.

To the homeless man or Viktor Frankl in Auschwitz every day becomes about surviving. They must contend with hunger, coldness and lack of shelter. Unlike western man they are not consumed by desirability or external endorsement. "Unless one is unconcerned by other people's judgments, has no fear of being disliked by other people, and pays the cost that one might never be recognized, one will never be able to follow through in one's own way of living. That is to say, one will not be able to be free." - Ichiro Kishimi

How can the capitalistic westernised man have so much and yet still remain unhappy?

The poets tell you to fall in love with another, but the existentialists and the Stoics tell you to fall in love with yourself. Be in absolute love with your own naked existence because you are blessed to be alive in this universe. Gaze into the night sky and ponder why is there something and not nothing. Maybe then you will appreciate who you are and what you have.

Your greatest asset is not your looks, your money or your achievements. No, your greatest asset, your greatest wealth, is that you exist in this dark recess we call the universe.

"Life is either a daring adventure or nothing at all." - Helen Keller.

When you get up and are in a pit of despair, do not look at the cars, the buildings, the roads or the people. Do not think of your failures or your mistakes. Dream of the innocent universe and how fortunate you are to be alive. Contemplate why there is something and not nothing. Think about that if there was no gravity, no water, no stars, no atoms, no strong and weak nuclear force, no kidneys or liver, no oxygen, that you would not exist. That we are alive is pure chance. That we can perceive our own reality is a miracle of Darwinian evolution. And we are only alive for a flicker of thunder. Be happy if only because you can be happy.

Gratitude is an extremely potent narcotic. Once you get a taste for your own freedom, your own experience and your own existence, nothing else matches. To be grateful, one must overcome narcissism, even basic narcissism for that matter.

Tie your self-esteem to the fact that you are alive in this despairing universe.

The greatest self-help book is inkless. It contains several blank pages that the reader uses to write down everything good in their "failed" life, everything they are grateful for. And if they are profoundly grateful, the first sentence would be: "I am grateful to be alive in this forsaken universe." You are your own psychologist. You are the author of your own perspective.

The terrorists of this world reside in your own soul. It is your own mentality that haunts you. The best psychologist in your life is yourself. Your own thoughts determine who you are.

Narcissism or nihilism, that is what one must choose between.

Trade your gratification for gratitude; trade your self-pity for self-realization; trade your fears for hope; trade your money for a wealth without money.

People say: "I need." "I need X, Y and Z to be happy." You do not. You already have everything. What is "everything?" It is existence.

You live and perhaps die on your choices. A man is but the summation of his choices. You are responsible for your reaction; you are responsible for your decisions. Your liberty is how you react to how the world acts.

Escape the cities, the blue skies, the relationships, the careers. Escape even what you love in this planet. Become one with the universe and you will discover the most serene tranquillity of all.

Being happy means disappointing people.

Van Gogh found peace when he looked at the stars. His life was tortured, and his paintings were not selling. But when he thought of the universe, he found serenity.

The atom is 99.9999999% empty. Therefore, you as a human are 99.9999999% empty too.

Man, either has time or money, but seldom the two together.

The universe resides in us as much as we do in it.

The illusory nature of life reminds me of Plato's the Allegory of the Cave. People only see what they are taught to see. They take the limits of what they have been brainwashed to see, to be the limits of the universe. What is unchaining them from the cave then, in this day and age? It is making them overcome their Economic Narcissism that only enables them to see life as work and relationships. Then the prisoner who returns to tell the other prisoners of the true world gets ignored and threatened. The other prisoners do not wish to know the true reality. Just like the billions who refuse to acknowledge the universe. They are so absorbed in what they see as true, that they do not want their illusions destroyed.

If you could compress the history of the universe into an earth year, modern human existence would only take place in the last few seconds of that year. That is how worthy we are.

One always remains a pupil if they do not listen to their own soul.

The best philosophy to have is to be the architect of your own philosophy.

The only thing worth finding is yourself.

The Dalai Lama, when asked what surprised him most about humanity, answered: "Man.... Because he sacrifices his health in order to make money. Then he sacrifices money to recuperate his health. And then he is so anxious about the future that he does not enjoy the present; the result being that he does not live in the present or the future; he lives as if he is never going to die, and then dies having never really lived."

Look behind you and you will see your shadow; look before you and you will see your dreams; but look into the universe and you will see your freedom.

There exists a schism, between the cosmetic meaning the economic system provides versus the true nihilistic meaning of the universe.

"Solitude is independence," said Herman Hesse.

Your duty if any should be to leave this world in a better place than when you first found it.

The life of a human is no more valuable than that of a farmed chicken and as you read this sentence three thousand have been slaughtered.

When you endorse yourself, you do not need external endorsement to be glad. To be unhappy because you are not liked is the greatest insult to the universe.

We are just an amalgam of electrons dancing in darkness.

I think, such is the capitalist environment that we grow up in, we misinterpret what being sociable means. To the insecure narcissist, it is understood to mean having forty thousand friends on Facebook and three million followers on Instagram. From a mature person's point of view, it means have three close friends, one or two close friends at work, a partner and that is all. Less is more. I have read it more than once, that those with fewer friends and people in their lives, more often than not are actually happier in their existence, than the social influencer with his or her followers in the seven digits.

The average man will produce 500 billion sperm cells during his lifetime. Now think of all the men that have existed since the dawn of mankind. Now think of all those sperm cells that never fertilized the egg. What is the moral? You are incredibly lucky to be alive. Start thinking about what a privilege it is to exist rather than what you need "to be happy."

This capitalist cancer infects our forsaken souls. It tells us to be obsessed with love, careers, image etc. One's existential freedom is provoked into action through severing the links with this obsession.

The failure is not that you are not liked; the failure is that you want to be liked. In wanting to be liked, you set yourself up to be accepted or rejected. The goal of Existential Nihilistic Therapy is to both make the individual aware of this and to encourage them to forgo it.

"The greatest discovery of my generation is that a human being can alter his life by altering his attitudes." – William James

The economic system of relationships and work is what makes one insecure and unhappy. In the future, hopefully, an alternative economic system prevails.

The dim light of a dying star is still better than no light at all.

They tell you to discover love, success, freedom, happiness etc. But above all else one should discover themselves.

The trick is to have the mind of an old person but the heart of a young person.

As the great film maker Stanley Kubrick said: "No matter how vast the universe, you must supply your own light."

Economic Narcissism is philosophical suicide. It is a means to have meaning in life, despite how corrupt that meaning is.

If you analysed a 1000 people you will find that 999 of them will have the philosophy where they wish to expose their identity to the herd be it a relationship or work. It is to be expected because they are brainwashed from youth to do so. Of that 1000 people, you might find one person who does the opposite, in that they try to prevent their identity from being known. That one person is someone who should be listened to.

The starting point of success is individuality.

Your freedom as Sartre or Frankl would attest is how you react to how the world acts. What distinguishes us as humans is that we can choose how to respond to what life throws at us.

One of the defining qualities that makes us human is our ability to override our instinct. But very few choose to apply this luxury.

Improving the world can start with improving yourself. We can make a difference in this world, no matter how miniscule, if we just change ourselves.

If you really want to learn something, let your curiosity do the teaching. We have too many machines in life. Students learn something twenty times so they can apply it the twenty-first time when a client or patient interacts with them. As such they follow the pages of a book rather than their own heart.

It applies to men as much as women. But take a naïve young woman. She opens a celebrity magazine and sees Kim Kardashian or Megan Markle, both of whom are dressed exquisitely and with their families. What does our naïve young woman think when she sees these celebrities? She thinks, "that is the dream life. I must get married and have children in order to be happy. I must look feminine and behave as women should behave. That is how I will become happy." The system advertises itself through itself. Mere Exposure Theory, Normative Social Influence and Social Comparison Theory all combine to make this woman immediately think she needs to be married to be happy. We see everyone else getting married and we instinctively compute that we need the same in order to be happy. Then our naïve young woman meets her friends for dinner to catch up. All her friends are married and have children and our naïve young woman is partner-less and childless. Because of this she feels left out. She feels that people think she is odd. This is the power of labelling. So our naïve young woman again instinctively says: "in order to be approved, in order not to be laughed at, I need to have a family." Now you must apply this to society overall. Those two threats are in part dictating how we behave.

Finding out what you cannot do is an important process of determining what you want to do.

Scientists still cannot tell us what initiated the big bang. Scientists still cannot tell us what initiated the first cell to form. It is thinking like this that makes one appreciate the fortuitous nature of life.

As Rollo May said: "The rebel and the saint are often the same person."

The universe is your teacher; it is your companion; it is your salvation.

If you can see the beauty in existence you will be happy.

The best things in life are free and being happy is one of those things.

As a human, you never cease learning and improving.

The number one fallacy of life is that we deny that we are an animal. The second great fallacy is that we are blind to the universe. There could easily be nothing. No films, sports teams, buildings, relationships etc. If a meteorite had not wiped out the dinosaurs there would be no love and careers. Thinking like that makes normal life redundant.

To paraphrase Oprah Winfrey: "Be grateful for what you have and you will be blessed with more; it is those who complain about not having enough, that never get enough."

There is no destination to happiness; the journey is the destination.

We only learn how to live when we grow old. The trick is to discover this luxury when young.

To love oneself is the beginning of a lifelong romance.

Individuality is success; it is looking left when everyone else looks right.

When you traverse through life with the mentality of appreciation or gratefulness you begin to take pleasure in the simple things and find that you no longer need the complex things to make you happy.

Man is caught in a bind: He refuses to conform and dies of starvation or ill health; he conforms, and he commits suicide because of the stress.

Why does matter, light, heat and time exist? Why is there something and not nothing?

So entranced, so preoccupied with life, that we ignore the vast dark ocean above and below us.

Do not go searching for more; appreciate your existence and let it seduce you.

The goal of these notes ultimately is to open the eyes of the reader. When you comprehend the universe or the miracle of the atom, the everyday dreams and worries become redundant. A woman once said my thoughts were extreme, but these extreme musings if properly applied can unburden you from the life of conformity. The current system is not one of bliss. One of the symptoms or by products is anxiety or unhappiness. My writings are an effort to show you the light of our dying star and make you appreciate this beautiful thing we call existence.

The Buddhist monks meditate to achieve ecstasy. They sit and relax and control their breathing and find a sedating warmness. The standard man in contrast can only achieve this ecstasy through being gratified. He has sex, he succeeds, he makes money etc. In order to feel something, he must do something. But your freedom is actually the ability to feel pleasure from doing nothing.

Going your own way, choosing your own path, can never be a failure. If you listen to your heart, you will not be misled.

"Every revolution evaporates and leaves behind only the slime of a new bureaucracy." - Franz Kafka. It does not matter what revolutionary book or film hits the market, for as long as education, urbanization and parenthood remain, the status quo will remain unchallenged and hence unchanged. The average child, in order to mature, must overcome about twenty years of indoctrination in the form of education, urbanization and parenthood. I am not suggesting such a mature child becomes a criminal; I am suggesting they become existentially liberated.

If you can make yourself happy through solitude, you will have acquired a potent skillset.

Compassion is being generous to the individual who cannot benefit you in any way.

The true tragedy of life is that we take it all for granted.

Becoming human is the most courageous thing you can do.

The universe can be for you or against you depending on your perspective.

You should set out each day with the determination to return a better man.

When was the last time you discussed the splendour of the universe with someone? Probably never.

Man is the tumour of this universe and economics is the tumour of modern-day man.

The real world is not the blue skies, love and careers. That is the illusion. The real world is the universe; it is the functioning atom.

Existential maturity, akin to Erich Fromm's dichotomy on love is not something you can just say to yourself or exclaim. You cannot just say you are mature. Existential maturity is something you must grow and cultivate, much like love.

A man must give birth to himself every decade; he must cultivate is own compassion for this universe; he must be the architect of his own renaissance.

You must love yourself, but not in a narcissistic method. The narcissist loves himself with respect to other people. He loves himself because he believes other people will love him or do love him. Existential maturity in contrast is where one displays an appreciation for their existence and thus loves the sensation of being alive.

We should measure people by maturity and not intelligence.

Despite all the crime and all the genius, the bold universe must toil. Nothing really matters.

They can take everything bar how you respond to them taking everything.

The universe is the most addictive drug of all.

It is not science or religion that will annihilate us. It is economics.

The current economic system has literally drugged society. The average citizen of this world does not see the galaxies flying through space or the electron dancing around the nucleus of the atom. What they see is love; what they see is work; what they see is money; what they see is sex; what they see is friendship.

To live is to suffer; to be happy is to find solace in that suffering.

Look into the atom and you will see truth.

"Youth is happy because it has the ability to see beauty. Anyone who keeps the ability to see beauty never grows old." - Franz Kafka.

Ironically, it is the individual that can be happy with nothing that can be happy with everything.

You are not born human; you must become human.

I read a piece about Einstein discussing how he developed his theories of Relativity (with General Relativity being the single greatest act or work of art that mankind has ever produced) and the author stated that in order for Einstein to produce those theories he (Einstein) had to escape in a sense from casual day to day life. Most of his peers in the scientific community were absorbed by what they saw day to day with their vision and that is why they failed to create what Einstein did. How could they, for all their calculations were based on what they saw when they drove to work or looked out the window in their office. Einstein started thinking beyond conventional life as we know it and started picturing a space rocket travelling at 90% of the speed of light and how it would measure a beam of light that was travelling beside it and hence gave us Special Relativity. He then distanced himself from Newtons gravity and saw how it is in fact space time being warped that causes planets to remain in orbit. Now he would not have been able to develop this relativistic theory of gravity had he just kept looking at apples falling from trees. He had to escape into the universe to see how it actually behaved. This is exactly what I am trying to conjure with these notes. You are so acclimatized to everyday life that you cannot see the universe. You cannot see the sun, the galaxies, the kidneys in your body or the atoms. You become hooked on what we deem normal life. It becomes about image, meeting expectations, money, conforming and with such a life accompanies stress and anxiety. What I try with these notes is make you see the universe; make you see the atom. Because when you do that the normal life of stress and anxiety becomes absurd and with this existential absurdity accompanies a simple appreciation for your existence in this world.

Right now, as you read these very notes, you are travelling at 67,000 miles per hour, because the very planet you inhabit is moving at that speed around the sun.

Does the futility of contributing to the economic system require suicide? No as Camus asserted, it requires revolt, freedom and passion. I would also add gratitude to that. When was the last time you woke up and the first sentence in your mind was: "How lucky am I to be alive in this universe?" Never I would imagine. Now why don't you think in such a nihilistic grateful manner? You don't because you have been educated since you were young to prioritize relationships and careers above anything else. You have been educated to be blind to the greater universe. Thus, to mature in an existential manner, you must rewire your brain.

The only way one can truly mature is through solitude. Bear in mind that when one visits a psychologist for an hour once a week, they are (the psychologist) essentially trying to recreate the conditions of solitude. The psychologist is really trying to be your voice of reason, telling you where you are erring.

Unless you understand the influence society has on you, you will not understand why you want what you want. We have no awareness into how presentation management (the desire to be labelled correctly) dominates our lives. A woman will more than likely marry a man who makes her look good in front of the herd. A man wants to be a successful millionaire for the same reasons.

What is drilled into the mind of the child is: "I can only be happy once I am liked." That sentence dominates their existence as they mature in an adult. That is why men desire to be successful and women desire to be beautiful. To actually be happy, one must overcome this.

You must see the positives in failure. In life you either succeed or you learn but you never fail.

Someday it will be man who will be bred as livestock to be slaughtered; it will be man who will be tested upon in the laboratories; it will be man who will be skinned alive to be made into a purse; it will be man who will be culled to control his population; and on that day, we will finally realize how worthless we really are.

The students who get top marks and a good degree, are the ones who repeat word for word and line for line what the lecturer says. This is also why they will die forgotten.

We take it all for granted and its only when we lose it all do we realize how good life is.

The only thing worse than not being liked, is being taken advantage under the guise of being liked.

One must recognise the enormous chance that has led you right to this moment where you are reading these notes. For some reason (and one that continues to perplex physicists to this day) more matter was created in the big bang than anti-matter. Then the four fundamental forces as well as Space-time are in existence that lead to the formation of stars. Then our parent star we call the sun is the right size in that it is not too big nor small. Then we must analyse earth. It just happens to be the right size, the right distance and contains the right chemical ingredients to enable life to flourish. Then the evolutionary biologists are startled by how the first cell came into existence and like the physicists have no answer as to why it did. Then through Darwinian evolution with the help of an asteroid life gave birth to an aquatic-animal that swam out of the ocean and evolved into land-animals. Then through another stroke of good fortune an animal evolved that could use language and with this skill gave birth to the very person who reads these notes. All in all, and this is very existential nihilistic, you are not meant to be alive in this universe and because you are not, it makes life so much better.

"A man wants to earn money in order to be happy, and his whole effort and the best of a life are devoted to the earning of that money. Happiness is forgotten; the means are taken for the end." – Albert Camus.

Live as if you are dirt famous. Live as if you are living in George Orwell's 1984.

The common individual is dictated by consumption. In order to feel gratified, they must succeed in some way, seduce someone or make money. They must achieve in life to feel content and this is precisely why they suffer. The pendulum swings between boredom and suffering.

Only the aristocracy suffer existential crises. This is where I diverge from many existential authors and therapists. Most people do not worry about the death anxiety because they are worrying about money and relationships and so on. That can be a good thing, in that it distracts from the death anxiety. But it can also be a negative, in that one becomes anxious and insecure.

The conformist lives in the future; the melancholic, in the past; the existentially liberated, in the present.

All the jobs, all the wars, all the sex, all the violence, all the money earned, all the tears shed, all the gratification gained, all are worthless relative to the universe. We cannot go on; we shall go on.

Sometimes I wish the universe did not exist, just so dog-fighting would vanish.

They can imprison your body but not your mind.

One would think that intelligence and maturity would be directly proportional to each other, in that as our intelligence increases, so would our maturity. In other words, the more we learn about the universe, harness new technologies and cure various illnesses etc. that we would become more mature. But this is not the case and it seems the opposite is true, especially in western society. They are as it turns out indirectly proportional to each other. As we increase our intelligence, we become less secure. For some reason despite our knowledge of the nihilistic world we become more embroiled in love and work and as I have remarked, those two things are enamoured with anxiety.

What matters is not the best living but the most living.

Life may be devoid of meaning but it does not have to be devoid of appreciation.

There are two ways to approach it: You can get angry at your failings or you can be thankful for your failings because in this cosmological island a failed life is still much better than no life at all.

"Never look back unless you intend going that way." - Henry David Thoreau.

There is a famous scene in the great film Dead Poets Society where Robin Williams character jumps up on a table and remarks: "I stand upon my desk

to remind myself that we must constantly look at things in a different way."
This is indicative of what I try to convey through these notes. We are so
acclimatized on normal life that we cannot see any other path. We would
have to take a trip to space and see earth from the perspective of the
universe to fully comprehend how meaningless our aspirations and anxieties
truly are.

Yalom is wrong if he thinks the death anxiety is the primary motivation of
the individual. In a lot of cases death is an escape from an unbearable
existence. They lost their job, their marriage broke up, they were convicted
of a crime, they are beset with a painful medical illness and so on, all of
which make them flirt with death. A million people commit suicide every
year because they want to die, not because they are afraid of dying. But you
can still apply existential therapy to their lives. If you awaken them to the
universe, and the illusion of life on planet earth and the fortuitous nature of
existence as a human being in this world, you can change their mentality.
They may still struggle, but at least they will struggle with a smile.

We feel a void in our lives, and we attempt to fill it with things like money,
possessions, and accolades. We think these things will make us happy.
When they do not or when the high wears off, we just seek more of them.
We become agents of gratification. Habitual life becomes about targets.
Gratitude is displaced and addiction takes the reins.

If prevention is better than cure, then change the economic system.

From a sociological perspective, you cannot have a good portion of society,
without a criminal portion of society. Counter-intuitively, crime actually
stabilizes society and you simply cannot have a society without crime. Even
if you imprisoned the 3% of those who commit crimes, that will just lead to
the remaining 97% committing crimes in turn themselves, and as such the
3% rate of crime would reappear. Similarly, one cannot mature in life
without first erring. You have no capacity by which to be a good person
unless you possess the capacity to realize that you can be deviant. You need
to suffer and make mistakes in order to actually grow. No person is moral
by chance, as in they are not born moral. The difference between those that
are mature and those that are not, is the fact that those that are mature
analyse themselves. They learn from their mistakes, and also to an extent,
from other people's mistakes.

We spend so much time planning this dream future that we live in the future at the expense of the present. We spend so much time looking at the top of the mountain that we forget that most of our time on earth is spend climbing the mountain and as such you must enjoy the ascent. The only happiness you find at the destination is the happiness you brought with you on the journey. To live for the top of the mountain is gratification. You say to yourself, when I have achieved this much, I will be happy. If you can possess a happiness on the journey, that is gratitude and it will still be there at the destination. It is the sides of mountains that sustain life and not the mountain top.

To every action is your reaction, and your reaction is what you do with what has been done to you.

It sounds so counter intuitive, but by knowing less people, one can become happier.

We are always in a state of dying. Dying to grow up, dying to succeed, dying to have sex, dying to make money, dying to be happy, dying to live and finally terminally dying. We live in the future at the expense of the present and as the saying goes, we ultimately die without ever having actually lived.

The irony is that the system that distracts us from the death anxiety (that is the meaningless universe,) actually causes us to feel anxious. It seems man is caught in an existential bind. He is the victim of anxiety in the economic system through stress at work and the problems in relationships. He then may turn to the absurd universe to reduce the scope of these thoughts but only finds more anxiety in the form of a nihilistic beast. What I try to do with these notes is make people appreciate this nihilistic beast. Like Albert Camus postulated, you may recoil in horror at such lack of intrinsic meaning when you gaze into the stars, but that does not mean you have to despair. The universe can be your death-sentence or if you allow it, your salvation.

I would hope in the future that existential nihilism will take precedence over sociological necessities.

We have sex education in schools, but why not have "solitude education." With such a mechanism we would teach students to learn to live in solitude, which would help them to mature.

We are the children of the universe. We are the consciousness of stars.

It is much better to have no money and be happy, than have money and be unhappy.

Nature did not intend to create us. We are mutation after mutation; chance after chance; epoch after epoch.

You have no leverage against a man that is content with nothing. Such a position is the royal flush of existence.

One must perceive existence as a gift. We should not be alive in this universe. If the fundamental constants of nature were different, life could not be created. If gravity were weaker or stronger life could not exist; if the speed of light was slower or faster, again life could not exist. So, the next time you wallow in pity over your failure to be in love or because you are not at a certain stage in your career, think about how lucky you are to exist in the first place. Make the most of this gift you have been granted and you can start by being grateful.

Trying to be liked by everyone in order to be happy is the most futile gesture. Firstly, because no matter how hard you try, some people will just not like you. And secondly, you will more than likely be taken advantage of. Counter-intuitively, in order to be happy, one must be prepared to disappoint people. They must have the courage to be disliked. "The courage to be happy also includes the courage to be disliked. When you have gained that courage, your interpersonal relationships will all at once change into things of lightness." - Ichiro Kishimi

You can thank the universe through appreciation. As Camus asserted, one must embrace the Absurd and you can do this by being grateful. There is no reason to live but equally so no reason not to, once you are alive.

Desperado, the terrific song by The Eagles, really cautions against living the life of excess.

The question of meaning (with respect to humans) is narcissistic because we are only an animal with language and without it, we would like all other animals be locked in a brutal war to survive. Language enables us to ask the absurd question, but it does not grant us the ability to answer it, not now at least. It does however enable us to understand the physics, chemistry and biology of the universe and from them we can deduce that there is no meaning to existence. One must ask themselves that when the constants of the universe (the speed of light; the gravitational constant, Plank's constant etc.) and the fundamental forces (gravity, strong interaction etc.) were decided by whomever or whatever, was man an intended by-product of those constants and fundamental forces? In my opinion I do not think he was. I think we are alive because of pure luck. Thus, it is narcissistic to assert that man has meaning because it assumes that man is superior to all other life forms on this planet (and universe), which we are not. We have just used the tool of language to make fantastic strides relative to all other animals. Camus's The Absurd is really a question of physics: Instead of asking "why man is alive," or "does man have meaning," one should ask why are the constants of nature and the fundamental forces the way they are? The person who can answer that will explain a lot.

Man has no meaning, but the universe may have. The economic system of love and work provides meaning for man but that is all just an illusion. The economic system is just a cosmetic meaning.

If you peeled off the skin of every human being, as painful as it would be, you could not distinguish the people from each other. Every man would look the same, as would every woman. We would not be able to tell the rapists from the geniuses. What you see when you look into the mirror is an illusion; it is a lie; it is a horrible deception. So, you are not this unique snowflake society has taught you to think you are. You are a pathetic useless collection of organs that happens to possess consciousness. Do not fool yourself and you are the easiest person to fool.

35,000 die from terrorism each year; a million die from suicide such is the economic system. We try to eradicate terrorism, yet the economic system is not challenged.

You only need two things to be happy. If you are reading these notes, you already possess one of them: Existence. The other component is Attitude, in that all you need is the correct mentality.

Maturity is an attitude, it is a mentality, it is a disease; unfortunately, so too is immaturity.

Reality is what happens while you are busy dreaming.

The more mature you are the more attractive you become and what is maturity in this existential sense? It is overcoming your basic narcissism that hides the universe from you.

To exist as a human being is not enough; man is condemned to make something of himself.

"The range of what we think and do is limited by what we fail to notice. And because we fail to notice that we fail to notice, there is little we can do to change; until we notice how failing to notice shapes our thoughts and deeds." - R. D. Laing

I would strongly recommend that young individuals live on perhaps 200 euros per week for maybe six months to a year because such a method of frugal living will make you appreciate the simple things in life more and will in turn will give birth to gratitude which will stand to you for the rest of your life. To learn to live with wealth you must first learn to live without it.

"The nitrogen in our DNA, the calcium in our teeth, the iron in our blood, the carbon in our apple pies were made in the interiors of collapsing stars. We are made of star stuff." – Carl Sagan.

There are hundreds of books that discuss winning people over or making them like you, but this is precisely why you are unhappy because you leverage your happiness on being endorsed by these people. Then there are hundreds of other books that discuss how thinking about success will procure success and again this is also why you are unhappy because you tie your self-esteem or happiness to being successful. My philosophy is to turn away from these things. In other word's you tie your happiness to the simple fact that you are alive in a world that had no intention of giving you a life. Hopefully, someday, you will reconcile being alive with the enormous chance that you are alive.

I cannot emphasize it enough: If you learn to live alone, you will have acquired tremendous skills with regards being happy.

We are not born insecure; we are made insecure. Logically if the sociological environment is what makes you defective, the solution is to distance yourself from the said environment.

Every day is a battle of likeability for the insecure individual. They spend half their lives asleep and the other half anxious. They worry about not being popular or attractive.

To put it bluntly, it is far easier to not be alive than it is to be alive. If the Permian or Triassic era had never ended, we would not be alive. If the earth were too close or too far from the sun, we would not be alive. If the earth were full of water or had no water, we would not be alive. So, stop asking what life can give to you and start asking what you can give back to life and you can do this by being grateful.

If you removed all the empty space in the atoms we are constructed of, the entire human race could fit inside the volume of a sugar cube.

If you do not have the strength and guile to change yourself, no one else will.

Despite your despair there is always something to be thankful for.

"Freedom is man's capacity to take a hand in his own development. It is our capacity to mold ourselves." - Rollo May.

"Finding the center of strength within ourselves is in the long run the best contribution we can make to our fellow men. ... One person with indigenous inner strength exercises a great calming effect on panic among people around him. This is what our society needs — not new ideas and inventions; important as these are, and not geniuses and supermen, but persons who can "be", that is, persons who have a center of strength within themselves." - Rollo May

One of the defining attributes of maturity is that one is always learning, always improving.

Society creates us. Freedom is creating yourself.

Dance with your existence and let it guide you.

The misuse of science in the name of economics is what will eradicate us. Man does not need protection from nature; man and nature need protection from man.

I know the reader will laugh at this assertion but go homeless for a week and you will appreciate what you do have. It is not that we do not have enough. We have too much and do not value what we do have.

The only difference between the prisoners and the free people, is that the former know they are imprisoned.

Happiness and people are indirectly proportional to each other. The more people you depend on to be happy, the less happy you will become.

You should never leave till tomorrow what can be accomplished today and being happy is indicative of that.

The mass of a neutron is 939.5654133 MeV/c^2. But, if the mass had been 939 MeV/c^2, stars would have blown up too early and the elements necessary for life would've never been formed. If the mass had been 940 MeV/c^2, then matter would not exist at all.

You cannot change what you did or what was done to you, but you can change how you react to what you did or what was done to you.

"The trick is in what one emphasizes. We either make ourselves miserable, or we make ourselves happy. The amount of work is the same." - Carlos Castaneda.

We are being stalked from the day we are born by death. Nothing you achieve and likewise worry about can abate this certainty. Thus, it is a most futile gesture to wait to be happy until you are closer to death.

We wait for the storm to pass when we should learn to dance under the rain.

Your substance to live should be because you can.

You are born an animal and it takes guile, patience and most importantly courage to become fully human.

Do not think about what you need; think about what you already have.

Your choices are never without consequence. Do it or do not do it, you always pay a price.

On the next clear night, stop what you are doing, go outside, stare into the stars and appreciate how good it is to be alive.

It is not happy people who are thankful, it's thankful people who are happy.

You must create yourself. You must find yourself. You must birth your own philosophy on how to journey through life. Do that and you will become mature.

Life may lack any purpose, but we must soldier on; we must go on.

There is no ten-step guide to happiness or a better quality of life. You either make yourself miserable or you make yourself happy, and no outside influence has a say in that.

I repeat myself on gratitude a lot, but I am only trying to emphasize that your attitude is the most important thing you possess, and the correct attitude is one of gratefulness.

The cusp of Existential Nihilistic Therapy (ENT) is worthlessness. The individual comes to realize how worthless life really is and if life is ultimately devoid of worth, then so are the individuals worries or anxieties. By teaching people that the universe is indifferent to them you can actually liberate them. You can make them existentially mature. "The only absolute knowledge attainable by man is that life is meaningless," said Leo Tolstoy.

If god really cared about us, he would save us from ourselves.

If the American Dream is so good, why do 90 Americans commit suicide every day?

The journey towards happiness is gratification; the journey is happiness is gratitude.

Philosophy, science and poetry convey how lucky we are to be alive, but this is suppressed by the economic system imposed on us that makes us insecure.

In one word I can sum up why every animal is alive today: Mistake. An error in its DNA replicating gave birth to its beauty.

Human beings are petrified of being independent and a large reason for the fear is that they are afraid of being negatively labelled by the herd.

The power of positive thinking, the one where you dream of success and life provides, is an appalling illusion. If positive thinking is true, why aren't we all millionaires and living the dream life. Statistically the only people who benefit from these corporate cults are the proprietors of them. It is a trick, a con, a psychological Ponzi scheme. The reality is that if success is living the dream life and being a millionaire, most people will fail. The capitalist system cannot support the majority, only the minority. My philosophy is not about being a millionaire before thirty. It is about being happy regardless of whether you have everything or nothing. It is about being mature because you recognise the truth of the universe. If I have learned anything in the study of existentialism and Buddhism, it is that you do not need much to be happy. You just must change the way you think.

People buy book after book pertaining on how to be successful in life and all they are doing is lining the coffers of the authors of those books. Most people will not succeed in life. But that doesn't mean you can't be happy.

If the speed of light were ten percent faster, life would not exist. The constants of physics are so finely tuned that if you change them slightly, life could not form. Now, when was the last time you ever pondered that nihilistic proposition?

Those who struggle against the system procure existential maturity. This says that those who conform implicitly to appease the demands of the herd are often insecure. Now that is not to say that everyone who conforms is immature. Of course, there are billions of people who are mature who conform. But there are also billions who are insecure because they are told to adopt the system unconditionally.

"I'll tell you something banal. We're emotional illiterates. And not only you and I - practically everybody, that's the depressing thing. We're taught everything about the body and about agriculture in Madagascar and about the square root of pi, or whatever the hell it's called, but not a word about the soul. We're abysmally ignorant, about both ourselves and others. There's a lot of loose talk nowadays to the effect that children should be brought up to know all about brotherhood and understanding and coexistence and equality and everything else that's all the rage just now. But it doesn't dawn on anyone that we must first learn something about ourselves and our own feelings. Our own fear and loneliness and anger. We're left without a chance, ignorant and remorseful among the ruins of our ambitions. To make a child aware of its soul is something almost indecent. You're regarded as a dirty old man. How can you understand other people if you don't know anything about yourself?" – Ingmar Bergman.

We betray existence in conforming unconditionally.

"If you haven't the strength to impose your own terms upon life, then you must accept the terms it offers you." - TS Elliot.

The number of people who go off travelling when young and return a more mature person is startling. They venture off by themselves and see the world and come home a different person.

The colleges teach students too much. They teach them that all that is to be learned can be learned from a textbook and consequently students forget that true creativity is earned by teaching yourself. The colleges as Noam Chomsky asserted are in place to fabricate a conforming class. They are there to produce obedient workers who will accept a terrible deal in working all their lives and will do so with a smile on their faces.

The tragedy for the individual is that in struggling to be one, they are negatively labelled.

We are engulfed in a battle from a young age: Cede to the tribe or defy them. You cannot run from who you were meant to be; you cannot run from yourself.

Far more hurt is done to the individual through psychological violence rather than physical violence. It is due to psychological hurt that we conform.

I cannot but help think the whole universe is an experiment designed by another intelligent life. Now they do not care about us. They did not intend for us to be created. We are an unintended by-product of the controls they put in place. But whenever I think why there is something and not nothing, I wonder where it all came from.

To do nothing, that is what man struggles so badly to do.

Do you think the vain celebrities of this world wake up and are perplexed by the strong nuclear force that binds the atom together and of which without it life could not form? No, they wake up and say: "How will I make money today?" or "How will I dress today?"

Human existence as Schopenhauer said is an error and I concur. Existence as we know it is error after error after error.

Everyone is a threat. That you do not see them as threats is how they operate.

You can be a soldier in life or a wolf.

Nothing changes because society never changes. Your fate is inextricably linked to society and what society does, you in turn do.

From the age of four our mind is educated in such a way that we learn to like ourselves only when we are liked by other people. We stake our self-esteem on being endorsed. Such emotional gratification only serves to make our lives a game of chance.

Visit a city where you are unknown and walk on its streets. That is freedom. Anonymity is freedom.

Existential maturity begins and ends with gratitude. Gratitude is the beginning, the middle and the end of happiness.

"Nothing behind me, everything ahead of me, as is ever so on the road." - Jack Kerouac.

You are if anything your response to the world. The only thing you can fully control is your response.

You can be imprisoned and be free; you can have "the dream life" and feel like you are in chains; perception is key to happiness.

Either you choose or society will choose for you.

"No man ever followed his genius till it misled him." - Henry David Thoreau.

The problem is that people equate living a good life with living "the good life" and they become desperate to taste it. What is this "good life?" It is being rich, beautiful, living in a mansion, having a family, owning fast cars etc. So many have bought into the capitalistic idea that happiness is wealth, when it is actually the reverse, in that your wealth is your happiness.

Personal Note

"The universe is change; our life is what our thoughts make it." - Marcus Aurelius.

From a personal note, what really made me mature is a combination of the following:

Be grateful: This is the most important skill you can possess to being happy.

Overcome narcissism: Instead of saying "I need," say "I have." Stop depending on people to like you in order to like yourself.

Embrace the isolation and lack of meaning: Teach yourself to live without people. Grow into the universe and the nihilism instead of running from it.

Accept your boredom: Overcome your need to be gratified every second of every day. Appreciate the small things. Appreciate your existence.

See the universe: Overcome your Economic Narcissism.

Limit being known: People through interpretation make us insecure. I am not suggesting that you completely avoid people. But minimize being known. Get off social media and so on.

Now there are other elements to it, but these would be the main points.

Final Word

"I see it all perfectly; there are two possible situations - one can either do this or that. My honest opinion and my friendly advice is this: do it or do not do it - you will regret both." - Soren Kierkegaard.

My notes are a failure. My notes are a failure within the current economic system. Man can never possess his autonomy if he is a slave to friendship, money and image. The things that supposedly give substance to life are the very things that imprison him. They make him insecure. Let's imagine there were two systems: The current economic system of work and relationships and a different system of pure solitude. Which do you think would be the most secure existence? It would be the latter. But people cannot see this, and secondly, they cannot see the stress associated with the current economic system. They are blind to how they make their lives more difficult through marriage and working. They are controlled by labels. The plastic surgery market which is worth billions is rooted in labelling. The psychiatric system too is influenced by labelling in that we see bipolar and schizophrenia and anxiety as things which must be medicated to eradicate their label. The narcissist too is murdered by labels. All in all, when man is labelled, he is stripped of his liberty. As shocking as it may seem, one cannot fully grasp their maturity by being labelled (known) because the very fact that you are known means your behaviour becomes controlled. Within the current framework, I see no end to the Capitalistic Insecurity. People will continue to suffer and continue to fail all because they must interact. At best all one can be is grateful despite the uncertainty. To mature in this sense, one must overcome their narcissistic brainwashing that instructs them to conform to be approved. Narcissism is immaturity. The narcissist is not aware of the universe. Life to such an individual is all about love and work. The atoms that constitute ones being, the galaxies, the kidneys in a human body, may as well not exist because the narcissist is passive towards them. The narcissistic individual in particular is devoured by love. Such a person is immature because of it, but this immaturity is part and parcel of the economic system and as such is extoled. For the insecure narcissist, marriage and maturity are mutually exclusive. Such individuals are so insecure that only one avenue of life is to be conquered and because of their inherent immaturity they do not possess the required skills to become a husband/wife or even a parent for that matter. In contrast (as I have alluded to in these notes) it is the very individual who doesn't see the necessity and importance of a relationship/marriage with regards their life happiness and esteem, that actually possesses the skillset to become married and a parent.

You must reconcile the beauty of existence with the chance of existence. Rich or poor, successful or a failure, you really must see how good it is to be alive in this universe. There should really be no life. It should not exist. There should be nothing and we are fortunate to taste existence. I find it hard despite these notes to put into words the feeling of being existentially free or existentially mature. From analysing myself it comes down to gratitude, appreciation and recognition of the true reality of the universe. Your existence should be your drug of choice. Life is not work and love. That is what the economic system has imposed on you. Life is gratitude and appreciation because when you think like that you recognise just how fortunate you are to be alive. The most frightening question one can ask is: Why is there something and not nothing? Why does the universe exist? Why do atoms exist? Why does life exist on what Carl Sagan famously described this "pale blue dot?" When you ask those questions, you gain insight into just how lucky you are to exist for there could easily have been nothing. No light, stars, planets, space, skyscrapers, city streets, houses, oceans and fields. Just darkness. Ultimately when you think like that, in such an existential manner, you can negate the economic worries that plague you. Society unfortunately instils in the individual that they must exist first and they then obtain maturity. The reverse is actually true. One must first grasp maturity and then they possess the skills to truly live.

Overall to be mature which ultimately means to be grateful which ultimately means to be happy, one must overcome their narcissism. It is the Economic Narcissism that is bred into humanity when young that blinds them to the universe. To be genuinely happy and truly free in this universe, narcissism must be defeated.

"Every one of us is, in the cosmic perspective, precious. If a human disagrees with you, let him live. In a hundred billion galaxies, you will not find another." - Carl Sagan.